WISE
ABOUT WASTE

WISE
ABOUT WASTE

150+
WAYS TO HELP
THE PLANET

HELEN MOFFETT

BOOK**STORM**

ISBN: 978-1-928257-68-4
e-ISBN: 978-1-928257-69-1

First edition, first impression 2019

Published by Bookstorm (Pty) Ltd
PO Box 4532
Northcliff 2115
Johannesburg
South Africa
www.bookstorm.co.za

Edited by Kelly Norwood-Young
Proofread by Sean Fraser
Cover and book design by mr design
Author photograph by Lara Aucamp
Illustrations from iStock and Shutterstock
Printed in the USA

For my parents,
Dinah and Rodney
Moffett (Moo
and Vos), shining
examples of green
living. Thank you for
everything you've
taught me.

And for Sean
McDonagh,
eco-theologian
and warrior.

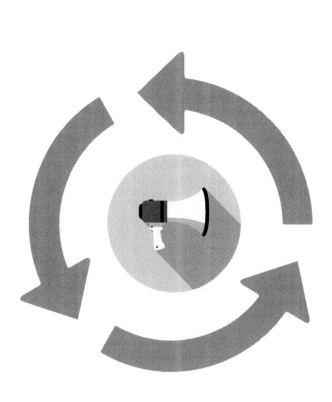

"I want you to act as if your house is on fire. Because it is."
Greta Thunberg, teenage environmental activist

"Never doubt that a small group of thoughtful, committed citizens can change the world; indeed, it's the only thing that ever has."
Margaret Mead, anthropologist

"The reasonable man adapts to his circumstances. The unreasonable man changes his circumstances. Therefore, all progress depends on the unreasonable man."
George Bernard Shaw

"Positive social change results mostly from connecting more deeply to the people around you than rising above them, from co-ordinated rather than solo action."
Rebecca Solnit, *When the Hero is the Problem*

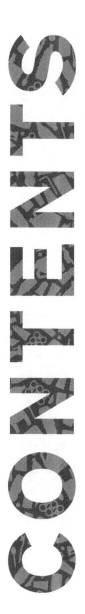

CONTENTS

INTRODUCTION

Writing a book on saving water was easy. Cape Town, the city I call home, was in crisis after three years of drought had emptied its dams. We faced the very real, very imminent fate of running out of water. The likelihood of having no water coming out of our taps focused everyone's minds (a polite way of saying there was mass panic).

However, the short-term solution to slashing domestic water use drastically was in fact straightforward. Although I rounded up more than 101 ways to conserve water (and there are lots more), the truth is that the middle classes simply had to stop pouring potable municipal water onto their lawns, into their pools, and down their toilets. If we stop doing these three things (which are completely insane, if you look at them square-on), much of the problem, ahem, evaporates.

The problem of reducing waste is infinitely more complex, and it's far more of a challenge to get people inspired to act. Capetonians could all understand the horror of a rapidly impending day when they would no longer be able to flush – a huge motivator. But it's much more difficult to jolt us out of our current thinking about waste, in a throwaway, consumer society that considers that if things are out of sight, they're out of mind.

The hardest thing about thinking about waste – and thinking green at all – is just how much thinking is needed. We have become universally addicted to convenience. We reach for objects – a light bulb, a toothbrush, a packet of biscuits – without stopping to consider the convoluted journey those things took to reach us via the supermarket shelves. There isn't time to think about where the raw materials came from, how they were manufactured, what they cost in energy terms to produce, then store, what labour was involved, how they are packaged (and why they're packaged that way), how they're transported to us, and how we will dispose of them once they've stopped being useful.

This book began when I took delivery of my brand-new rain-tank. This great tough thing, designed for an outdoor existence, arrived entirely encased in plastic wrap – as if it was made of porcelain. At the same time, my publisher watched *Blue Planet 2*, and, like almost everyone else who saw it, was horrified at the impact of plastics in the ocean. So she thought a handbook that gave tips on how to eliminate plastic from our lives would be a good idea, and I thought a book with ideas for a "waste-free" lifestyle would be even better.

For nearly 15 years, I've been rather smug about sending no more than five or six kilograms of solid waste a year to landfills. So I thought (naïvely, it turned out) that I had a head start, some basic tips I could usefully share. Then I started the research and promptly fell down a rabbit hole – into a warren of enormous dimensions and complexity.

The problem of waste is far bigger and much scarier than the megatons of plastic bobbing around in our oceans. Thinking about waste means coming to grips with the damage we've done to the environment.

To get the frightening bits over with quickly:

→ Carbon dioxide released into the atmosphere by our addiction to and economic dependence on fossil fuels is heating the planet to levels that are melting the ice-caps, leading to sea-level rises with the potential to wipe out the planet's low-lying cities. The carbon dioxide trapped in the atmosphere is also making climate and weather dangerously unstable. We've seen more storms, cyclones, hurricanes, droughts, runaway wildfires, heatwaves (and resulting deaths) in the last several years than humanity has faced in the last ten thousand years. These events have always been part of the planetary furniture, but there are now too many of them, and they follow each other so swiftly that there isn't time to recover and rebuild before the next catastrophe strikes. This carbon dioxide is not the same as air pollution: it's invisible, but it's the most dangerous and life-threatening form of waste we need to address.

→ We're living through an age of mass extinctions of other living species – plants, insects, reptiles, birds and other animals, thanks to habitat destruction (clear-cutting forests so that fast-food chains can make more burgers, companies can print more advertising flyers or make five-ply toilet paper) and poisons like insecticides. In the past, this has often generated false "either/or" thinking, with the old adage that "bunny-huggers" care more about pandas than poor people.

The truth is that life has evolved as an extraordinary balance between all living creatures – from the microbes that break down leaves and rocks into soil in which we grow crops, to the big predators at the top of the food chain – of which, unfortunately, we are the most dangerous, not just to others, but to ourselves. Urban as we have become, we have disconnected from the reality that in order to eat, we need to *grow* food (it can't just be miraculously made in factories). And to do that, we are utterly reliant on a network of insects, birds, bacteria, soil, water and climatic conditions that urgently need to be protected and preserved so that our children don't starve. Our waste is recklessly punching holes in this network: this is why those pathetic photos of seabirds, seals and turtles strangled by plastic bags deserve our attention.

➔ In treating the ocean as a toilet, we have forgotten the basic, life-preserving principles of photosynthesis and oxygen/carbon dioxide exchange. Humans and animals are able to breathe because we live in symbiosis with plants that soak up carbon dioxide and produce oxygen. More than a quarter of the oxygen in our atmosphere is produced by tiny ocean phytoplanktons (algae, diatoms and other single-celled organisms), which also regulate atmospheric carbon. If we kill off these microscopic creatures, we're on course to die particularly horrible deaths. What's even more apocalyptic is that these oceanic oxygen tanks aren't likely to die off slowly, but to collapse suddenly and catastrophically. And yet we dump poisons, rubbish and sewage into our oceans at the same time as we strip them bare of anything we might be able to eat or sell, disrupting the self-regulating mechanisms that keep the sea healthy with all its organisms in balance.

So you can see why researching this book often induced horror and despair. The shift caused by the industrial revolution of the late eighteenth and early nineteenth centuries profoundly changed the shape of global cultures, as civilisation and development were twinned with economic growth based on manufacturing rather than agrarian (food) production. But it was the consumer culture of post-World War II capitalism – in which we started treating the resources of the planet as both infinite, and infinitely disposable – that really created a monster. What's worse is that Western cultures have sold a vision of big cars and junk food and expensive branded goods (most of them unnecessary) to almost every country and culture in existence. We treat the planet as a vast ATM that we can draw from forever.

The awful truth is that our global ATM balance hurtled past zero a while back. We're in overdraft, and even if we stop extracting right now, this minute, it will take strenuous efforts by the next few generations to pay back the debt we've incurred. What's more, we're drawing on these finite resources to produce and buy stuff we often don't need, and then we hurl that same stuff back into a void where someone or something else will whisk it away so that it doesn't inconvenience us.

One thing is clear: we have to do something, and we have to do it now. But it's complicated. Effective ways of reducing waste are tricky to boil down into life strategies, partly because of all the contradictions and complexities: electric cars, for instance, may not use petrol, but they're often indirectly reliant on coal; we might be recycling our milk bottles, but then they need to be washed – and that takes water. We need to eat less meat, but while veganism may be the humane option, it's not always the most environmentally friendly one in semi-arid and arid countries where humans rely on ruminants to process grass and tough vegetation into protein (see p. 96).

In addition, the middle classes are constantly being told what steps they should take as individuals to reduce their footprint on our groaning, battered planet (our ONLY viable home). But there's also a whole bunch of research that says that individual efforts count for nothing, given that only about a hundred big corporations are

But surely there are maps to lead us away from this lemming-like rush to the edge of an environmental cliff? The short answer is yes. Here is the basic mantra greenies have been chanting for decades now – excellent guidelines for waste-wise living:

reduce, re-use, repair, repurpose, recycle.

However, the environmental activists who believe that these steps are coming far too late to save the planet have new r-words for the ways we need to live:

refuse, resist, revolt, rewild.

The advantage of the first set is that they involve principles everyone can follow. The second set we can at least think and talk about, and use as political levers.

And there are more r's, according to environmental researchers: the buzzword "sustainable" is already past its sell-by date. Instead, we need to be thinking:

restore, rehabilitate

(see 'Can this planet be saved?' – p. 131).

responsible for 70% of all carbon emissions; that only ten rivers (all in developing countries to which the West ships its waste) are responsible for over half the plastic flooding into the world's oceans. And that at this crucial tipping point we've reached, only drastic, immediate action by governments around the world can save us from ever-increasingly catastrophic climate change.

Very few countries (notably Costa Rica and New Zealand) have stepped up to the plate by insisting that the environment is a priority in terms of budget and legislation, although there are promising signs that others will follow suit: for example, Scandinavian countries are divesting from fossil fuel industries; China is investing heavily in solar energy. Some UK and US politicians and activists are starting to speak of a "Green New Deal", in which a "green industrial revolution" will be launched not only to save the planet, but create jobs. But it all looks frighteningly like too little too late.

Even just reducing plastic waste is a lot more complicated than it seems: all the alternatives need to be researched. If we're replacing plastic with paper, bamboo, glass, cloth, what are the environmental impacts of these substitutes? And close scrutiny of (over)packaging brings into focus that products are packaged for the convenience of the vast chains that flog them to us. And, as many eco-warriors have insisted, the onus (and pressure) needs to be on manufacturers to stop this at source, rather than relying on us to recycle them at the end of the chain.

Every solution poses new problems: organic foods and humanely farmed meat might be better for the planet and healthier for us, but they're costly, and how can we possibly exhort poor people to eat more expensive food? Which takes us right back to the heart of the problem: the systems that produce our food, fuel our economies and organise our labour forces are unsustainable, alienating and inhumane in the first place. I kept reaching this point as I did my research where I'd have to put my head between my knees.

To return to my first conundrum, can individuals make a difference? Yes and no. We need corporations to stop their insane, headlong pursuit of profit at all costs; we need governments to rein them in, instead of allowing them to pillage and pollute shared resources like air and the oceans for free; we need investment and infrastructure in decent, safe public transport and energy from renewable and clean sources; we need brand-new economic models that involve income cycling through societies rather than accumulating (see 'The radical, unpopular and downright weird stuff' – p. 115). These projects are big and daunting, and it's hard to see how, for instance, boycotting single-use plastics will have an impact.

In the past, we've spoken about climate disruption and the trashing of the planet as if these have "just happened", when the reality is that a small handful of extraordinarily wealthy and powerful people have driven this process. This horror story has real villains, who have gone faceless and nameless while leading the rest of us along their lethal path. For example, it was fascinating to learn that when the plastics industry first took off in the 1970s, the thinking and legislation were that businesses that created these plastics would need to be responsible for cleaning them up – an expensive process. Enter powerful corporate lobbyists who rapidly got governments on board, if not in their pockets, and soon the burden of plastic disposal shifted to individual consumers – if they could be bothered.

These people – who overlap with the 1% who brought down the world economy in 2008 because of their reckless gambling to make yet more profit, who are among the 0.1% who have billions upon billions lying rotting and useless in tax havens – need to hear the rumbling of tumbrils in the streets.

Still more astonishing is that the rights of these few super-billionaires to hoard and hide truly obscene amounts of money, to fund climate change denialism, to lead governments by the nose, to encourage or enable fraud and corruption, are defended by huge numbers of people who are certainly not sharing the benefits: whose pensions are shrinking, who are struggling to keep up with inflation, who are staggering under debt.

But shrugging and continuing on our merry wasteful ways isn't an option. The air we breathe and the water we drink, the food we eat (which affects our health and our children's health) depend on us making strong efforts to change our consumptive (pun intended) ways. When I see a toddler scampering to the deli fridge and tugging out a bottle of Coke while his yummy mummy smiles proudly, when I see able-bodied adults demanding plastic straws to drink from water glasses, I realise how much there is that individuals can do, and still need to do. Capetonians learned that individual efforts CAN make a significant difference, when, by cutting our water consumption by nearly 40% in a matter of months, we helped head off Day Zero and stopped our taps running dry in the nick of time.

Still, thinking about all this is daunting. Where do we start and how do we stay motivated if everything is so terrible? Several years ago, Simon Gear wrote a book, *Going Green: 365 Ways to Change Our World*, in which he pitched an interesting angle – that of self-interest. By that, he didn't just mean keeping the planet habitable for us and our children. He reckons that going green will, in the short-term, be:

→ good for your marriage and family
→ good for your health
→ good for your pocket.

Given that many associate switching to green lifestyles with pious austerity, sacrifices and the loss of comfort, what I liked about Simon's approach was that he makes it clear that there are immediate benefits – BIG ones – to practising greener principles.

Let's unpack his ideas a little.

HOW IS GOING GREEN AND REDUCING WASTE GOOD FOR YOUR MARRIAGE AND FAMILY?

First, let's turn this on its head. Living together in small communal units (of which a family is the most usual) obviously saves resources. A family of six, for instance, needs only one fridge and stove (never mind the vacuum-cleaner, washing-machine, stepladder ...). Divorce means doubling up on everything, including expensive household appliances. Simon argues that a happy, strong marriage is ultimately good for the planet.

But does it work the other way round? Can a green lifestyle build stronger domestic ties? It seems that the answer is yes. This is especially true if we factor children into the equation. Food historian Michael Pollan has noted that one of the most effective solutions to the USA's obesity crisis AND its waste problem is for families to cook their evening meal together, from scratch.

Learning to cook is one of the greener things you can do (see 'Food', from p. 89, for more on this), especially if you make economical meals as opposed to scattering caviar over your lobster. But more than that, getting the whole family to put together a meal is a bonding exercise, as is sitting down to eat together.

Avoiding waste as a family involves constant discussion and negotiation, and it's one way that parents can teach children, but also be taught by them – young people, as we've seen from the massive protest campaigns by teenaged environmentalists, are keenly aware of green issues. Even if the tiny things you can do as an individual feel like spitting in the face of a tsunami, they model responsible and ethical choices and actions to our children – and that's no small thing.

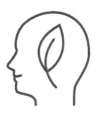

One of the busiest families I know (the parents are medical professionals; their daughters have a hectic schedule of after-school and homework activities) cook dinner as a team almost every night. It's a near-sacred ritual. There is always a main course, salad and a modest pudding, even if it's just fruit and yoghurt. The children dress and toss the salad and lay the table. Phones are put away. Everyone sits and holds hands for a minute. Then they eat and talk. Everyone has to tell one story from their day at work or school. If anything good happened, this is shared and celebrated. Once dessert is finished, the children scramble up, but the adults linger over coffee or wine, make plans and discuss schedules. Phones are then fetched and diaries updated.

This family is noticeably happy. Everyone is affectionate. And no one is carrying extra weight. But how is this green? And what does it have to do with waste?

The truth is that humans are consumers. We can't all go and live on a mountain top and swallow snow and inhale mosquitoes like hermits of old. So the trick is to consume mindfully – to get the maximum bang for our buck in terms of nourishment, pleasure, relaxation and social connection from our meals (or whatever else we are consuming), while generating as little waste and drawing as gently as possible from the earth's resources in the process. If your family is gulping takeaway burgers or microwave meals while hunched over screens, generating a sack of Styrofoam containers, crumpled napkins and plastic cups that go into a dustbin along with the leftovers, you're not only planting your heel on Mother Nature's neck; you're likely setting yourself up for long-term health problems and family alienation.

HOW IS GOING GREEN GOOD FOR YOUR HEALTH?

Let me count the ways … there's another entire book here. From walking or cycling to the shops to save petrol, to eating more home-grown and home-cooked veggies; from watching the scenery go by on the bus or train instead of raising our blood pressure in rush-hour traffic, to breathing air and drinking water less laden with chemicals and poisons – this one is a no-brainer. Our water, our air, our seas keep growing filthier. Food systems are broken: they operate on principles of profit rather than nourishment, so soil is becoming depleted and sterile, and our food less and less nutritious, if not downright unhealthy. Plastics in micro-form have penetrated all our food chains, and having that stuff in our bodies is NOT good for us – it's associated with auto-immune diseases, infertility and a variety of cancers.

On the other hand, contact and immersion in natural spaces (parks, woodlands, wetlands, mountains and more) is good for our physical and mental health – not just a hippie idea, but proven. There's a lot of research supporting this; one interesting piece showed that prisoners in a maximum-security lockup were less violent, depressed and likely to use drugs when their cells looked out over a forest than if they overlooked a concrete courtyard.

An environment is the space that we live in, that shapes us. It's not a green space "out there" lived in by rare animals and occasionally visited by the rich in search of recreation. It is what surrounds us and gives us life. The healthier it is, the healthier we are.

HOW IS GOING GREEN GOOD FOR YOUR POCKET?

If you had to draw a Venn diagram of tips on both waste-wise living and saving money, the two circles would overlap almost entirely – or they should.

I visited an exhibition in the UK called "Make Do and Mend" that zoomed in on the many ways that people recycled, re-used, patched, darned, cobbled or just plain went without during World War II.

But these habits have become lifestyles that belong in a museum, quaint things our grandparents did, in the face of rampant shiny capitalism that demands that we buy something new every five minutes, and chuck it when it falls apart ten minutes later.

We need to return to a way of thinking in which being frugal and thrifty are seen as vital and ethical lifestyle choices – as well as plain common sense. There's a huge difference between being generous and being wasteful, and we sometimes get the two confused.

But there can be a whiff of Marie Antoinette playing at being a dairymaid when the middle classes cinch in their belts. It's all very well suggesting virtuous "mend and make do" tips when the poorer citizens of this country and indeed the globe already practise these through sheer necessity, and find no pleasure or satisfaction in them.

However, it's a valuable exercise to consider what steps you'd take if you simply couldn't afford new clothes, pre-packaged and prepared meals or takeaways, a thirsty 4x4, bottled water, and a flat-screen telly – none of which are necessities. How much would going without these really affect your quality of life?

During the Western Cape's water crisis, not a few township residents told me, "Ja, now you have to live like we do" and the basic principles – living like your grandparents did, or your neighbours in the township next door do – remain the same.

While a great deal of thrifty practise is time-consuming, it can also be soothing and even sanity-saving. Simmering soups made with the cheapest fresh veg from the market and home-grown herbs, stitching up a drooping hem or darning a favourite pair of socks, spinning down to the shop on a bike, bartering plants, picking fruit, sharing

I once rhapsodised to a friend about the time I took a small gas stove to the beach and ate steamed mussels fresh off the rocks. She flinched: when she was growing up, her father's salary never stretched the entire month. So the week before payday, the family would head for the beach in the afternoons to forage for food. She shudders at the memory of abalone (a delicacy poachers literally kill for), mussels, crayfish and other seafood "luxuries" – because she associates them with privation.

what we have: in a world that seems to grow nastier, colder and more crass by the minute, these small actions are good for our mental health. They're also very good for the planet.

Equally important, the next wave of job creation is going to include precisely this kind of mending and making do. Repurposing, servicing and repairing goods is already the focus of many NPOs in southern Africa; projects like these should become mainstream sources of employment. (See 'Consuming' – p. 47, and 'Home and family' – p. 77.)

So going green is good not just for the planet and future generations, but for you, your loved ones, your community, your pocket. But there is another element of self-interest here: putting green principles into practical action is an important form of preparation for what the future might hold.

When Cape Town almost ran out of water, panic led to punch-ups in supermarkets, as people squabbled over supplies of bottled water – largely because, thanks to a spectacular failure on the part of the city and the snoozing media to sound the warning bells, the news came as a shock to many. But those who had been reading the writing on the wall (or rather, watching the dam levels) for several years already had water-storage and saving devices in place. The drought has now broken, but I still live off the water grid, even though lugging buckets is getting old: because it's a set of skills I know I'll need again in the near future, and I don't want to lose it. And even if you don't need to live off the contents of your veg garden or run your car on home-made biofuel in the immediate future, consider this: your children may very well need to know how to do these things.

The other attraction is that green living has a huge overlap with ethical living. Over a decade ago, when wrangling with climate change sceptics, British actor and writer Stephen Fry pointed out that even if climate change was a hoax or greatly exaggerated (and it isn't), we will live better lives – more humane, less wasteful and greedy, more mindful of others – if we green up. I believe that it's a balance between these two guiding principles – self-interest and kindness, or what might be called simple human decency – that will keep us on track as we go into an uncertain future.

HEAD START

One thing that's needed if we're going to be wise about waste is the ability and flexibility to change our ways of thinking. We need to get wiser in general. Making changes to our actions and habits starts in our heads, so our first task involves shifting mindsets. Here are some tips to help us prepare mentally for a waste-wise lifestyle.

1. **Step up to the plate.** In spite of the terrifying data pouring in about the state of the planet, the impact of runaway capitalism, and the failure of governments around the world to address the single greatest danger we have ever faced – the loss of our habitat – I still believe Margaret Mead's words: "Never doubt that a small group of thoughtful, committed citizens can change the world; indeed, it's the only thing that ever has."

2. Yet as an individual, you could live frugally, recycle everything, go off the electricity grid and walk everywhere, and all the energy savings you might make would be a drop in the ocean set against the damage done by one coal-fired power station in one minute (or any other big, energy-guzzling business). The problem with staring this in the face is that it renders us despairing and helpless. **Do not be overwhelmed.** Resistance is NOT futile.

3. So what can we do as individuals when the problems are so vast and need such massive structural and economic transformation before we can even stumble towards solutions? It comes down to the simple mantra we already know: **think globally, act locally.** To which I'd add this very important rider: **act both as an individual and in concert with others.**

4. First, accept that **there is no such thing as a "zero-waste" or "waste-free" lifestyle**. We all generate waste, as we breathe, eat, drink – from the carbon dioxide we exhale to the biological wastes our bodies produce. Even the disposal of our mortal remains after we die presents a problem (see pp. 121-22). The trick is not to add tons of industrial by-product,

especially in the form of carbon dioxide and plastic pollution, to our planetary footprint.

5. Becoming waste-wise means shifting our mental habits, and becoming aware of and alert to our consuming patterns. **We must change our "out of sight, out of mind" attitudes to waste.** It's not enough to diligently throw our chip packet or soft-drink can into a litter bin: we need to think about where that packet or can comes from in the first place, and what resources (labour, fuel, water, space in a landfill) its onward journey will cost.

6. Understand that **you will have to swim upstream** – like a spawning salmon – against the tide of popular culture and mass marketing (at least at first, although things are changing, and fast). Become a salmon. Embrace your inner fish.

7. **Prepare to research everything.** Take nothing for granted ever again. Google is about to become your best friend forever, and even then, double-check what it leads you to. Do NOT fall into the trap of believing fake news, conspiracy theories and simplistic claims, not even when they tell you what you want to hear. Use fact-checking sites like Snopes and Africa Check to verify what you read online.

8. **Don't waste time arguing with climate-change denialists or "sceptics"** any more than you would with flat-earthers or apartheid apologists. These are not simply well-meaning but misguided individuals: they are on the wrong side of science, history and truth. I'm all for respecting the rights of individuals to hold differing opinions, but wilful ignorance cannot be excused, nor should we engage with it.

"Climate change denial is not just ignorant, it is malign, it is evil, and it amounts to an attempt to deny human rights to some of the most vulnerable people on the planet. The evidence about the effects of climate change is incontrovertible, and the moral case for urgent action indisputable." These are the words of Mary Robinson, former president of Ireland, and head of the Elders, a group of world leaders (founded by Nelson Mandela) who fight for human rights. She goes on to say: "Climate change undermines the enjoyment of the full range of human rights – from the right to life, to food, to shelter and to health. It is an injustice that the people who have contributed least to the causes of the problem suffer the worst impacts of climate change ... We have entered a new reality where fossil fuel companies have lost their legitimacy and social licence to operate."

The evidence of climate disruption, as a result of global warming, is clear. Almost all scientists agree that the planet is in serious trouble, but because of the persistence of climate change denial (often paid for by fossil fuel industry PR, just as tobacco industries went on spending billions "disproving" the lethal effects of smoking for decades after they knew it was a killer), a great amount of time, money and effort is being wasted proving what we already know: that if we go on pumping CO^2 into the atmosphere at our current rate, it will disrupt life and "civilisation" as we know it. To keep denying climate change, or to suggest that short-term economic gains are worth sacrificing a planet for (the line taken by, for example, those advocating fracking or strip-mining of coastal dunes), is as evil and immoral as denying the Holocaust. There is no "other side" of the story that has to be presented for "balance", any more than there is "another side" to the theory of gravity.

That said, there are many shades of grey (or green). This does not mean that evidence of environmental catastrophe is some huge con, or that "it's not all that bad". It means that our understanding of the many complex issues involved is incomplete. We may find some of the changes we make have hidden environmental costs we haven't yet grasped. Some decisions have to be balanced against other urgent environmental factors: during Cape Town's water crisis, for example, friends who were using cloth nappies for their babies had to switch to disposables to get their water consumption down to the prescribed 50 litres a day. We may find that nature regenerates faster than we dare hope – the areas surrounding Chernobyl that had to be evacuated following the nuclear meltdown there were repopulated by wild animals, including bears and wolves, none of which have two heads, within a decade or two. We're all on a vast learning curve.

9. **Avoid red herrings**, such as "the earth cycles through periods of cooling and heating, what is new?" In the past, short of meteor strikes and volcanic eruptions, these kinds of fluctuations took place over thousands of years. Now they're happening too fast for many species to adapt. Knowing that the planet has suffered through five previous episodes of mass extinction (the most well-known of which was the wiping out of dinosaurs) hundreds of millions of years ago is not much comfort or help at this point. What's happening now, in terms of loss of species, is not "natural"; it's catastrophic.

10. **No, the problem is not overpopulation.** All green activists will hear at some point: "It's not that the earth doesn't have enough resources; there are just too many of us." (I'm always tempted to ask these folk what they propose doing about all the "extra" people that doesn't involve mass murder: shipping them off to Pluto, perhaps?) *Yes, there are indeed too many of us* – to all have a four-bedroomed house with two cars in the garage.

Worldwide, those in the top 10% in income earned consume 48% of the world's resources each year. Poor communities often present and face very real problems when it comes to waste disposal, but the truth is that those whose lifestyles are modest do not present the most pressing environmental challenge.

It's when cultures that prize large families overlap with middle-class lifestyles that we have a problem. However, for argument's sake, let's agree that we need to stop having more than two children per family (unless we're adopting). Even if we could do this (few things make people more hot under the collar than prescribing family size), the practical implications make up a labyrinth that could swallow this entire book.

Why? The World Health Organization has published figures over the past five decades showing that to shrink family size involves one powerful step: educating women (as in literacy and numeracy). No other intervention comes close, not even all the social engineering tried by some Asian countries in the latter half of the twentieth century. The next most effective strategy for limiting family size? Building societies in which women are considered fully equal citizens, and not just on paper. And that means societies in which everyone has easy access to decent, free reproductive health care, not just the cheap and nasty solutions thrown at poor women. This care includes accessible and safe abortions. You see? I've already offended swathes of people and alienated certain religious communities, including members of my own (I'm Catholic).

And yet the logic is undeniable. Those who huff and puff about poor women having large families are often those who have no problem with halting funding to thousands of non-profit family-planning clinics all over the developing world. Until the men in those communities have vasectomies or commit to condoms (and they still have to lay hands on these), what are the women supposed to do? It's as if the rich (not so) secretly believe that the poor have no right to sex, much less the pleasurable, anxiety-free kind.

I am tempted by social engineering as a shortcut: in my dream world, every man who has a vasectomy should be given either a small lump sum in cash or a small tax rebate for life (women too, but it's much cheaper and easier to sterilise men). This could be a double win: at the same time as arresting their capacity to produce mouths that need feeding, men could get a bit of capital to start up a micro-business, finish building a home, and so on.

11. **Understand that the advertising industry lies.** Spectacularly and shamelessly. We do not need many of the products we have been led to believe are necessary to our comfort and happiness.

At the end of the twentieth century, big businesses and the advertising industry, flying in the face of all environmental principles and common sense, decided to flog us: big luxury 4x4 vehicles in which to run down to the shops or cruise around the suburbs; bottled water (in countries where tap water is safe to drink – even though it takes up to 26 litres of water to bottle, package and transport one litre of bottled water); and fabric softener. All these are murder on the planet, and not one of them is necessary. Billions of tons of resources have been used to make them, and they have generated many more billions of tons of waste that is difficult or impossible to extract from the air and oceans into which we have dumped them.

Similarly, a few years ago, we were presented with coffee capsules, which we embraced enthusiastically, in spite of the fact that they're an environmental nightmare and also utterly unnecessary (there are half a dozen ways to make decent coffee at home that don't involve putting indestructible trash into landfills). Some brands did indeed start making (expensive) biodegradable pods or capsules. But the point is that we buy into the latest trend just because it's a trend – and without counting the cost to the planet.

12. Another reason to practise small green habits: if we're filling up ecobricks and sorting our waste into recycling containers, there will come a moment when we'll ask, **"Why are manufacturers cramming all this rubbish down our throats in the first place?"** Or, as one British blogger pointed out tartly, if she had to fiddle about with a mooncup to stop her tampons washing into the sea, why were industries allowed to get away with dumping tons of poisonous waste into the ocean? This motivates us to start pressuring politicians.

13. If marching in the streets doesn't appeal, **donate to the organisations that DO mount political campaigns.** There are many excellent ones. British comedian Mark Watson has a green "swear jar" – every time he breaks one of his own green rules (forgetting to take his re-usable bags to the shops, leaving his PC in standby mode, using the lift), he puts money in the jar and donates it to Greenpeace at the end of the month. If you can't donate, join an online petition site and support it. My one of choice is Avaaz, which reports back to its global community and constantly agitates for environmental reform.

14. **Your green habits need to be context-specific.** In some countries, you have the option of choosing a green(er) energy provider (while we're stuck with Eishkom for the foreseeable future). Many European countries allow only hybrid taxis to operate in bigger cities. In the UK, there's a movement to boycott internal flights, and for train, coach and bus companies to step up the quality of their service. We may not have these options, but we have others. Find out what's do-able for your community and locality: for example, in Barbados, which has a glorious climate and iffy roads, many drive 4x4s – but mostly in the form of small, open-topped, fuel-efficient jeeps.

15. **Brace yourself for criticism** – often, sadly, from other greenies. It can be very disheartening being told that your solar panels are made of environmentally unfriendly materials, or that

electric cars still require charging and therefore run at only one remove on fossil fuels. Say politely, "Thank you. I'll research it further," then change the subject. But do follow up on that research.

16. **Develop a strategy.** It's no good vaguely intending to live a waste-wise life; as with the water crisis, have family meetings, where everyone comes up with one or two concrete examples of things they can do. These can range from cutting down on excessive showering and hair-washing, or not leaving computers on all day and night, to composting, to learning how to knit, cook and sew. Draw up "feel-good" principles to practise: for example, for every new item of clothing purchased, another item has to be given away or handed down. Have "clear-out" days, when your older children are encouraged to give away the stuff they don't need.

Things to do as a family that are green AND fun: walking the dogs (or even just all going for a walk); having a big bake or cooking spree on the weekend that produces bread and biscuits, soup and sauces for the rest of the week; having an hour a few times a week when everyone has to switch off their gadgets, put down their phones, and play games like Scrabble and General Knowledge.

Look for forms of entertainment, especially as a family, that don't soak up electricity or cost a lot. If someone in the family plays a musical instrument, for instance, make this a part of regular recreation. Drawing, painting, crafts, knitting and crocheting, chess and other board games, book clubs: find something that works for you. If you're going to spend money, rather do so on making memories with family and friends than trawling the malls.

Create gadget-free hours, evenings or days. These have the added benefit of greatly reducing your stress levels. I'm not Jewish, but ever since hearing about the concept of e-sabbaths, I've practised them regularly. You'll find that one day a week away from electronic devices comes as a relief.

17. South Africa has the worst Gini coefficient in the world, according to a World Bank report covering the years 1994–2015. This is a fancy way of saying that we have the biggest gap between the rich and the poor. It feels wrong seeing a silver lining here, but it does mean that **there is almost nothing you have that someone else won't benefit from**. There's nearly always a charity or non-profit that can use your goods, clothing or even your recycling. Pick a local NPO(s) or charity to receive your decluttering items (see 'Resources' on p. 148). Many shelters will fetch your goods, for free.

SAVING ELECTRICITY (ENERGY) AND WATER

Electricity, especially in South Africa, which uses especially "dirty" (polluting) coal to keep our power stations running, is a huge sock in the planet's eye. Here the self-interest principle is clear: as our power supplier has been run into the ground in the last decade, electricity costs have risen to eye-watering levels. **Saving electricity = saving money AND the planet.**

Some pundits say this will cause the same scenario we saw in Cape Town's water crisis – that with greatly reduced consumption, municipalities and state providers have less revenue for maintenance and upgrading. I'm afraid I'm hard-pressed to shed a tear at the thought of less money going into Eskom's corruption-stripped coffers. The other principle at work here is that if we use less electricity, there's less drain on the national grid, and we're less likely to be hit by power outages. Plus, when they do come, we'll be better prepared for them.

18. **Get into the habit of switching off all appliances at the wall instead of leaving them on standby mode.** Did you know that microwaves use more power overall keeping their digital clocks going than by cooking our food? In case of what Eishkom euphemistically calls "load-shedding", having our gadgets switched off at the walls also means that when the power fails or surges back on, there's less likelihood of frying the electronics involved.

19. **Solar lanterns:** not just for sitting outside on summer nights. Mine is an excellent substitute for a reading light or bedside lamp.

20. **Use low-energy light bulbs**, but dispose of them responsibly – never throw them in the bin, but take them to a collection point; most supermarkets provide these.

21. Batteries need recharging and are also a headache to dispose of safely. But **there are alternatives to batteries:** remember wind-up clocks and radios? You'd be surprised at what you can find in camping shops, but we need to push for items like these to be more generally available – and inexpensive.

22. **A lot of small gadgets can be recharged simply by soaking up the sun** (LED lights, radios, torches, etc.). I'd love to see this option for laptops, tablets, cellphones and the like.

23. If you have the capital to install one, **a solar geyser is a marvellous green option** that will slash your electricity bill, sometimes by as much as half.

24. If you can't afford to go solar, **get your existing geyser lagged or insulated**. You can even do this yourself: there are special "geyser blankets", but you can manage with old blankets and lagging, even tinfoil and string.

25. **A solar photo-voltaic (PV) system is a very good idea in sunny South Africa** as it can generate electricity for part of or all your home. Remember the alarm when we were told we would have to "register and pay for" our solar geysers? If you are planning on installing a solar photo-voltaic (PV) system, you do need to register this and get a certificate stating that it doesn't pose a hazard. This is no different to getting an electrician's certificate when building or selling your home; it is simply a safety check, given that electricity can kill, or start a fire. It is not (so far) a sneaky means of taxing us extra.

26. Heating presents a major problem for environmentalists in the northern hemisphere, but down south, we should NOT be apeing these lifestyles by putting expensive heating in our homes. The same goes for cooling systems: with very rare exceptions, South Africans do not need air-conditioners and underfloor heating. Rather **insist on building homes that are cool in summer and warm in winter** – designing them for best use of sunlight and air. In Nice, where the summers are baking, medieval buildings have cunning systems of vents that circulate air – still a boon centuries later.

Green homes are not the stuff of science fiction. Ten years ago, on a visit to Stanford University, I was struck by how many of the houses in the surrounding suburb, where residents were both wealthy and green, had been built on off-grid principles. They featured sod roofs, vertical gardens and veg beds, water collection devices and grey water plumbing, solar PV systems in the form of Tesla walls (essentially huge solar-powered batteries) so that the owner could plug their electric cars into the house for recharging with sun energy.

A little further north in Marin County, homes had rainwater tanks and nets for harvesting dew and fog, composting toilets, roofs covered in solar panels, gas-generating compost "digesters" and more.

We may not be able to make these sorts of changes right away, but the single biggest energy-saving step we can take in our homes is to install solar geysers and insulate our ceilings.

27. Not everyone can rush off and build the perfect green house. One good halfway measure is to **put insulation in your ceilings**. This helps keeps your living space cool in summer, but traps heat in winter.

28. **Home heating:** the priority should be any room in which a baby, or someone elderly, sleeps. Investigate the options – electric radiant heaters gobble electricity (and can't be left unattended). Wall panel heaters are a good choice. An electric blanket switched on for an hour before bedtime raises the temperature of the room by several degrees, and uses little electricity. I swear by hot-water bottles, because they're portable, and my mama's crocheted covers keep them toasty for hours. Jetmaster or similar indoor stoves burn wood (but this is still an improvement on coal-burning smokestacks), and new models use astonishingly little: careful engineering means that five or six small logs can keep your home warm all evening, and the chimney is very good for spreading the heat through the room or house. Some models have small stove-tops, so you can simmer soup or boil a kettle on top of them – very handy during power blackouts. You get double green ticks if you burn wood from cleared alien trees.

29. **The most eco-friendly means of heating: warm clothes, woolly socks and slippers, thermal undies and hats.** Americans who sublet my home while I was on sabbatical complained bitterly about how cold it was (in September): "It's so bad we have to wear sweaters and scarves indoors!" Well, yes. That is one way to deal with chilly interiors.

30. Unless you're caring for those whose clothing and linens need daily laundering, **you don't need a tumbler-drier in South Africa** with its hours of daily sunshine: hang your clothes out to dry. Use wooden, not plastic pegs (when these fall apart, the spring goes into the metal recycling jar and the peg bits into the wood-box). If you live in the Western Cape, with its wet winters, invest in a drying rack.

31. **Cook on gas.** Note that gas stoves and the piping to the cylinders need to be installed by an approved supplier, to reduce the (very tiny) risk of blowing yourself and your neighbours up. Rooms in which gas heaters and stoves are used also need to be well ventilated.

32. And now for **saving water:** see *101 Water Wise Ways!* The resources list (p. 154) suggests places to buy this.

CONSUMING

(HOW TO BE A LESS HUNGRY CATERPILLAR)

Once again, let's get the grim stuff out the way upfront. I realise that pointing this out is not going to win me friends, but we need to accept that **capitalism has failed**. This is nothing to do with communism, socialism, or any other political system (after the US, the most "capitalist" nation in the world at the moment is China, officially a Communist country). The pros of capitalism (which has given millions unprecedented amounts of freedom, choice, comfort and leisure, as well as high standards of living) simply can no longer outweigh its biggest con: that its underlying principle – that resources are unlimited and must be extracted in endless pursuit of "economic growth" – is rapidly rendering the planet a place incompatible with peace, stability, security and ultimately, life.

"Growth!" "The economy!" "Jobs!" shriek the politicians and the corporates, bent on extracting a few more years of profit at any cost from unique, life-sustaining ecosystems that have developed over millennia, and which will take centuries to heal from our depredations. Worse, few of the projects dangled in front of us as "job creation" do what they promise: offer secure employment at decent wages and with safe working conditions, other than for a very small group at the top of the heap. Don't take my word for it; ask the Marikana widows.

Besides, this is not an either/or scenario: there are models of economic growth (job creation with an emphasis on processes, not products; investment in renewable energy sources; emphasis on vocational training and skills to boost circular and repair economies) we should have switched to decades ago. As a species, it's not that we need to ditch growth; rather, we need to accept that we picked a destructive and ultimately deadly mechanism to deliver that growth.

But that's the bigger picture, and this is not a tome on economics.

Nevertheless, we need to rethink the way we slot into this picture of extractive growth and the great capitalist machine, given that we all purchase goods.

To state the obvious, to generate less waste, we need to buy less stuff in the first place. Minimalists have a phrase for the ways in which we relate to and store physical objects: "organised hoarding". At the beginning of 2019, everyone went mad for Marie Kondo's decluttering TV series, but what this revealed was a simple truth: we need to stop accumulating so much stuff. (On the subject of Marie Kondo and her principle of keeping nothing that does not "spark joy": the socialist and artist William Morris beat her to it 140 years ago when he said, "Have nothing in your houses that you do not know to be useful, or believe to be beautiful.")

This is where the "think globally, act locally" mantra can really pay off. Start in your own backyard. Buying produce and goods with minimal packaging, and that create jobs in your neighbourhood, as well as offering different and alternative economic models, even on a tiny scale, is one way to help.

So before you shop, here are some alternatives to think about.

33. **Sign up for a community exchange system.** These are often a source of information about alternative and cashless economies. They can be a bit laborious to deal with, and for a good range of offerings, it's best to pick one that offers regular markets. You may have to wade through dozens of offerings of long-distance angel Tarot readings (which may indeed be what you're looking for), but I've found my local one an excellent source of plants (especially edible ones), fruit and veg, and books. They also offer platforms for donation and barter. See 'Resources' (p. 148).

Community exchanges are always context-specific: for instance, an older widow in a small rural community used hers to offer baby-sitting in exchange for handyperson services (strapping younger folk to fix her leaking taps, or crawl into the attic to lag the geyser, etc.). This was because everyone knew each other, so there was a trust system in play.

One that operated in Manhattan acknowledged that exchange systems couldn't pay for rent, utilities or medical bills, so it focused on three main forms of offerings – bodywork (aromatherapy, shiatsu, etc.); design and word-work (setting up websites, designing posters, editing and proofreading); and art (paintings, pottery, interior design advice). This meant that people counting their pennies could still afford a few luxuries – a relaxing massage, a beautiful painting – on an exchange basis.

34. **Bartering: social media has made this much easier.** We now have electronic platforms for specific goods; we can include photographs, check out the individuals offering stuff, etc. I've stocked three veg gardens almost entirely via barter.

35. **Freecycle.** The interesting thing is that this now-global initiative (an online club in which folk offer goods for free on a first-come, first-served basis to others in their neighbourhoods) started in Tucson, Arizona, for one reason only: to keep things out of the city landfill, which was filling up at an unmanageable rate. Now people use it as a means of "shopping for free" and disposing of unwanted goods that might still be useful to others. See 'Resources' (p. 148).

In his book *Mongo*, Ted Botha explores the concept of putting out unwanted goods on the street the night before refuse collection day so that others can help themselves: a practice seen in cities like New York, and countries like Japan and the Netherlands. Ted set himself a challenge: furnishing his entire East Harlem apartment only with what he could find on the streets. And he did it, too, proving the truth of the adage that one person's trash is another's treasure.

36. **Shop at home:** whether it's a tube of half-used hand-cream in the bathroom cupboard, forgotten tins and jars in the pantry, or the clothes we've packed away, get into the habit of scouring what's available in your own storage spaces before going shopping.

If going waste-less is costing you a bomb, then you're doing it wrong. I read two pieces in popular women's magazines about doing without plastic – for a week in one case, and a month in another. In both cases, the authors simply went online to find re-usable and plastic-free replacements for everyday household goods – at faint-making prices. It was the 70-buck toothpaste in a glass jar that boggled my mind, given that you can pop a mix of bicarb, salt and peppermint oil on your toothbrush, wet it, and clean your teeth for pennies (see Tip 99). Instead of ordering "green" substitutes for plastic or disposable items online, use the internet to find out how to make your own, or repurpose what you already have.

37. Our frenzy to buy, buy, buy stuff, almost all of it on credit, seems a particularly stark sort of madness in the light of our waste problem. Remember the World War II poster during a time of petrol rationing: "Is your journey really necessary?" Without becoming killjoys, we need to ask: **"Is this purchase really necessary?"** Shopping should be something we do out of necessity, not for entertainment.

38. **Be wary of consumer events like "Black Friday"** (imported from the US and shoehorned into our lifestyles). Instead of running up debt, make events like sales and special offers work for you (I live close to the last department store in South Africa, and twice a year they have half-price sales at which I stock up on pure wool socks for my diabetic dad). If you're on a tight budget and have been saving to replace an elderly household appliance like a fridge or stove, or need to buy uniforms or sports equipment for your children, then waiting for a commercial event like Black Friday becomes a good strategy.

39. **Resist obsolescence**, as well as purchases made for the financial benefit of big banks and cellphone companies. We've heard about the scandal of Apple secretly and deliberately making its older phones run slower to prompt users to upgrade. Likewise, far too many replace their cars every five years because this is how payment plans and warranties are most profitable for the sellers and the banks – but not for the consumers, and much less the planet.

40. **Vote with your wallet.** I've switched to shopping at a biggish chain that doesn't, to be honest, always offer the best quality or the freshest produce. But nearly all their fruit and veg is loose, as opposed to prepacked, unlike other big-name chains, where you have fewer options for packing veggies into your own bags. On the other hand, the big-name chains sometimes have wider (if pricey) organic and free-range options.

41. **Investigate your local markets.** These need not just be the hipster kind, attended by folk with artistic beards dropping quantities of cash on hemp coffee: there might be a small market garden close to where you live. The best cabbages I ever tasted came from a township community garden that sold its surplus to a small organic shop in my suburb.

42. Pick waste-saving, healthy shopping styles: ordering organic boxes, picking your own veg, and more. Share news of your favourite waste-wise markets or shopping spots – and remember that this can even be the local branch of a big chain, if they sell their goods loose and encourage you to bring in your own bags and packets, or if they're making efforts to cut down on packaging. If you have a car, keep a special box in the boot with containers, bags and jars for visiting waste-free shops.

What's in your backyard? I'm lucky: in my immediate neighbourhood, I have:

→ A Low-impact Living café and shop that supplies dry goods and veggies loose or in bulk. Shoppers can buy fruit and veg, nuts, pasta, spices, household cleaners and other goodies scooped out from vast plastic drums and glass jars, on a BYOC (bring-your-own-container) model. If you run out, you can help yourself from a cupboard of empty jars.

→ A Neighbourhood Farms shop (at my nearest hospital), where the vegetables are grown literally on site, using rainwater stored in tanks, costing the planet absolutely nothing in terms of food miles to transport or store.

→ A tiny, pick-your-own vegetable garden that's open on Saturday mornings.

→ A farm stall where locals can arrange to sell their fresh goods (I take my lemons to barter) on weekends, and which is the only place I can find cucumbers that aren't encased in plastic.

→ A juice bar that gives a free smoothie if you drop off your glass jars for the use of their customers.

→ An organic salad farm that offers weekly veg boxes.

The message here: find what green shopping initiatives are just around the corner from you, and then (this is vital) support them.

43. **Make household goods and gifts from scratch** (clothing, condiments and other food items, accessories, toys and more). As well as cost- and planet-saving, this is immensely satisfying. Also see 'Celebrations and festivals' – p. 101.

Some things are indeed tricky to make at home. I've tried manufacturing my own bath soap and candles with disastrous results (hint: the entire candle is not supposed to burst into flames), and no matter how hard I try, I've rarely been successful at making bread with yeast. A friend who bakes bread and brews beer with panache can't master cheese-making.

However, some things are so laughably simple, quick and cheap to make, you'll slap yourself for ever having bought them in the first place: into this category goes peanut butter (all nut butters, in fact), mayonnaise, cottage cheese (also labneh and paneer), tomato pasta sauce, chilli sauce, granola and muesli, spreadable butter, body and hand lotion (even moisturisers), most household cleaners, laundry detergent, toothpaste.

Taking just a little bit more skill, but also relatively easy and cheap (and not time-consuming) to make: yoghurt, stock, many baked items (including muffins, cupcakes, pancakes, fruit cake, soda bread, biscuits and brownies), chutney, pickles, kombucha (and other fermented food and drink), jams, liqueurs, ice cream, certain sweets. And a little more expertise will have you baking your own bread, pies and cakes, whipping up samoosas and roti, making your own butter, brewing your own beer and wine.

44. Writer Diane Awerbuck has come with this set of **guidelines for plastic replacements**, and in fact for ALL the goods we buy:

→ Is it made from a renewable resource?
→ Is it biodegradable, or can it be easily and cheaply recycled?
→ Is it durable – a piece you'll keep and use for years, if not decades, perhaps even as an heirloom?

45. Finally, **buy green:** The Lazy Environmentalist is a website (also a book, TV and radio series) that lists the greenest brand of every possible item, from a kayak to a kitchen knife, for American consumers. Here in South Africa, Twyg offers a similar service, at least for clothing and food purchases, as well as information on planet-conscious consuming. See 'Resources' on p. 148 for details.

46. **But beware of "greenwashing"**: simply slapping the word "eco" or "earth-friendly" onto soothing packaging with a fern or panda design does not make a product green. Always check what qualifies that product to make such a claim (Google is your friend).

Simply slapping the word "eco" or "earth-friendly" onto soothing packaging with a fern or panda design does not make a product green.

RECYCLING

Because recycling differs dramatically from area to area and from community to community, rather than giving detailed guidelines on recycling (which would amount to another book), you're urged to research exactly what's available locally.

Some small or rural municipalities offer no recycling facilities; a friend who lives in a small Karoo town packs her car to the roof with rubbish to drop off for recycling every time she makes a trip to the city. Sadly, in some small rural townships, no functional waste removal or disposal services are provided at all. Farmers and others who live in rural isolation are used to dealing with every scrap of their own garbage: for 30 years, my parents disposed of their own sewage, grey water and trash – a complex system involving a burn bin, a midden, a septic tank, multiple compost heaps, and the resident pig.

However, waste processing and recycling offer cash-strapped municipalities a revenue stream, and the opportunities for job creation are obvious. An entire employment sector needs to open up around recycling.

47. How your neighbourhood or municipality goes about recycling or waste processing depends on numerous factors: from the local climate, to the location of landfill sites, to the presence of recycling depots and green NPOs – even the local wildlife. I take my glass, paper, tin and plastic to Oasis, an NPO in the Cape Town suburb of Lansdowne that offers intellectually disabled adults safe employment, and includes recycling as one of its income-generating activities. Check out whether you have similar options near where you live, or **find out whether your suburb offers a recycling pick-up** along with regular garbage collection. Mine does, although we haven't yet got to the stage of some North American and European suburbs that require residents to recycle by law.

I was fascinated to see that in many rural American communities, where almost everyone has their own car, waste removal is done on a DIY basis. When I lived in a tiny town in Maine, we had to take our garbage to the local dump and pay to drop off anything that went directly into the landfill, but pre-sorted goods for recycling could be put into the appropriate containers for free. Small depots paid money for glass and tin, with the option of donating these amounts to a charity you could choose from their list. One reason for this system? In the days when anyone could toss anything onto the local dump, it turned into a location for bear free-for-alls: bad for the bears and dangerous for the humans.

In Switzerland, it's against the law to send your rubbish out of your district; municipalities and individuals therefore have to deal with all their own garbage, in a country in which littering is almost a hanging offence. This makes citizens think very carefully about the waste they generate. We can learn a lot by comparing waste disposal and recycling systems in place in other communities and countries – there is no one-size-fits-all model.

48. As a rough rule of thumb, **you should be able to recycle clean paper, glass, tin, metal, many forms of plastic**. (The "harder" the plastic, the more easily it's recycled.) Your local municipality should offer detailed instructions on what can and can't be recycled; ideally, this information should be online.

49. **Tins, plastic containers, and so on, need to be reasonably clean before recycling,** but we shouldn't be using drinking water to wash them. I wash out milk bottles and empty cans with water pumped from the washing-machine – just enough to get the gunk off. No need to rinse.

50. **Electronic waste** – in the form of old computer towers, monitors, cables, laptops, tablets and phones – is particularly burdensome, as some of the materials are difficult and dangerous to recycle. However, the good news is that outfits that repair and redistribute these (usually to schools in poor areas) will often accept your donations. Ask your nearest computer store what your options are. In the meantime, resist the idea that we need to "upgrade" our electronic devices all the time. We do NOT need a new cellphone (or tablet, or laptop) every year, no matter how irritating the reminder calls and texts are.

51. While some South African cities have good recycling facilities that allow for a wide range of materials to be recycled, others rely heavily on "informal recyclers" or waste-pickers, who scour through garbage for collectables and recyclables they are then able to sell to recycling centres. **Support waste-pickers rather than complaining about them.** You can help by sorting your recyclable waste before putting it out on garbage collection day – that's if there is no local recycling pick-up option.

Waste-pickers (or "reclaimers") are often marginalised and harassed (including by police and security guards), even though they are responsible for South Africa's unusually high levels of recycling, especially of plastic waste. Surely it would make sense to formalise this as a form of job creation. Municipalities and communities should work alongside those prepared to do this work, to ensure their safety and hygiene, and provide them with storage facilities and protection from harassment.

52. **Is burning an option for disposing of waste?** The jury is still out on this one – it's not the greenest option; it requires space and exceptional care and vigilance, especially in my home city, which has dry summers, strong southeasters, and a history of disastrous fires. However, for paper and cardboard stained with food (sugar/flour/maize packets, pizza and cake boxes, used paper napkins) and more intimate bathroom waste (pee paper, used cotton-wool and dressings, panty pads, and such-like), it's the quickest and cleanest option. I have a burn pit in my garden, and shovel the resulting ash into the compost.

This feels normal to me because my parents lived for decades on farms or smallholdings where they were responsible for their own garbage disposal. Although they composted, buried bones and dog poo in the midden, and endlessly re-used containers like jam jars and yoghurt pots, they still had to burn what remained.

So burning waste feels familiar and non-threatening to me, but if you want to follow this route, proceed with extreme caution. Do it on a windless day, and have both a fire extinguisher and a big bucket of rainwater on standby. Never ever leave the fire unattended, not for one second. Once everything has burned, empty your bucket of rainwater over the ashes, then follow up with a few spadefuls of soil. Stay home for the next hour or so, and check that all is quiet before leaving the property, especially if the wind picks up.

Burning waste feels familiar and non-threatening to me, but if you want to follow this route, proceed with extreme caution.

PLASTIC AIN'T FANTASTIC

A recent headline asked: "Is plastic the new fur?" According to *National Geographic*, almost half the plastic on the planet today has been produced since 2000. That's less than 20 years – the lifetime of our children – to generate, among other things, the Great Pacific Garbage Patch, a floating island of plastic three times the size of France – and that's just one of the many islands of plastic menacing the seas.

Yet it takes three or four CENTURIES for plastic to break down – and when it does, it degrades into smaller and smaller pieces, which are much harder to extract from the sea and soil, and easily enter the food chain. In the meantime, demanding (or rather, passively accepting) that our goods come swathed in plastic has turned our seas into killing zones, and our landfills into toxic zones (because plastic doesn't biodegrade, it has to be burned, which renders it exceptionally nasty). This doesn't sound good: "PVC and halogenated additives are mixed into plastic waste and their incineration leads to release of dioxins and polychlorinated-biphenyls into the environment." (This is from an excellent blog on the impact of plastics on our environment by Rui Xing of the National University of Singapore – see 'Resources' on p. 154.) This is one reason Asian countries are starting to turn back container-loads of plastic waste exported from Western countries for "processing" – i.e. dumping.

When I first charged out, rattling my sabre at plastic waste, I was soon reminded that **while we are producing way too much, plastic has its uses**. It is both light and tough, it reduces food waste (which is not only wicked in a hungry world, but wastes massive amounts of water in turn), and it has important hygiene benefits. Sample factoid: since fish started being packed in plastic rather than paper, incidences of food poisoning via fish have dropped.

So not all plastic has to go. But if you're shopping and your purchase comes in plastic, try to pick the kind that's re-usable. My freezer is a cornucopia of plastic containers that once held products like yoghurt or margarine – the unofficial version of Tupperware.

Then came the laborious business of researching the environmental impact of each alternative to plastic. As I wailed to a friend that using paper instead of plastic meant thinking about how that paper was manufactured, how much water was used in the process, how best to recycle it later, she pointed out that **a paper bag doesn't end up in the ocean** – and if it does, it's unlikely to choke a turtle to death, enter our food chain, or pollute someone else's shoreline.

So while we're not going to ban plastic entirely from our lives and homes, here are some of the ways we can cut down on it.

53. **We all know we need to stop asking for plastic bags when shopping.** But how often have you got to the supermarket till and realised your re-usable bags are at home or in the boot of your car? And what to do about those rustly plastic bags we put our onions and apples into before having them weighed? The trail-runner Karoline Hanks has designed little fabric pouches that clip onto your handbag or belt with a carabiner. They are small enough that they never get in the way, and out of them, like rabbits from a magician's hat, emerge three tough but light shopping bags made of parachute fabric, and two lightweight cloth veggie bags. She also makes waxed fabric that substitutes for clingwrap and sandwich wrap. See 'Resources' on p. 154 for how to get these and similar products.

54. What's with the plastic bag in which chain pharmacies seal your medicines before putting them in a wire basket and then locking with a cable-tie? **Ask the dispensing pharmacist to put your medicines straight into the basket, or to use a paper bag.** And if they have to lock the basket (heaven forbid that your 'flu meds might make a bolt for freedom), why not use a padlock that the cashiers all have a key for? (A bouquet to Dis-Chem: since I started this research, this chain has stopped using plastic dispensing bags, thanks to consumer complaints – all hail the power of grumbling!)

55. **Kudos to the bookstores that will gift-wrap (in paper) but refuse to give out plastic bags.** Also those countries and districts that have legislated against plastic bags. I notice that some branches of an upmarket local chain no longer sell plastic

bags at all – shoppers who haven't bought their own bags have no choice but to buy re-usable ones. (Obviously, this assumes a certain level of affluence.) On the other hand, many till packers still reach automatically for plastic bags, especially those flimsy ones, for products such as meat or fish. You need to head them off at the pass. I use separate bags for chilled or "wet" products, including one made from recycled pet food bags that has a wipe-clean interior.

56. **There's a big debate about plastic straws** – with many restaurants barring these and now offering bamboo or metal straws. However, there has been vehement pushback from disability rights activists. Plastic straws are indeed a boon for the elderly and some disabled people (I used them after a fall in which I smashed up my teeth), but they were invented to deal with the new post-World War II milkshake culture. Next thing, they were showing up in all cold beverages. My question is, why are you using straws AT ALL, if you're able-bodied? They're obviously a huge help for those with permanent or temporary disabilities, or who need them for reasons of age or infirmity, but this business of bringing a healthy adult a drink with a straw in it needs to stop.

Once again, common sense and kindness rule: some plastic items (straws, tampon applicators, those gadgets that allow one to chop onions or peel eggs one-handed) are extremely helpful to those who are temporarily or permanently disabled, including with conditions as everyday as arthritis.

57. **Stuff small bits of single-use plastic into two-litre milk containers to create ecobricks** (visit the Two Oceans Aquarium website for everything you need to know here – see 'Resources' on p. 154 for details): this has the added benefit of compacting together lots of little bits of plastic that are particularly lethal to ocean fish and birds, and very hard to extract once in our water systems. Ecobricks are also good for absorbing materials that are otherwise very hard to recycle: clingwrap and medication packaging, for example.

58. Another good reason to give up smoking: **there is no way to recycle cigarette filters,** which retain poisons and aren't biodegradable. If you must puff, then roll your own ciggies.

59. **In the supermarket, check the small print**: Is the packaging really recyclable? Can it be recycled here in South Africa, or in your municipality? A lot of smaller municipalities have little or no recycling capacity (something that needs to change, as this is a potential source of job creation and income-generation for cash-strapped municipalities – see p. 58). Ratepayers need to get active on these matters (see 'Citizen activism: working together for change' – p. 125).

60. Toys: by definition, these are items that will be outgrown, and **almost every plastic toy you buy will eventually end up as part of landfill – they are notoriously difficult to recycle**. Here in South Africa, we have hundreds of crèches and playschools to donate used toys to, but thinking ahead, we should be making toys (knitting or crafting) or buying them second-hand. Charity shops can be an excellent source of vintage or preloved toys, and craft collectives often make wonderful (and racially representative) dolls and other toys (also see 'Celebrations and festivals' – p. 102).

CLOTHING AND TEXTILES

Clothing is becoming a growing waste problem. Although it's re-usable by definition (or it should be), we have to do our usual homework when choosing clothes, shoes, accessories and textiles. For instance, we think of cotton as "natural" and therefore a green option, but more insecticides and fertilisers are poured onto it than almost any other commercial crop in the world.

Plus, we may have to **rethink our attitudes to leather, silk, and even (gasp) fur**: if these forms of apparel are humanely and sustainably farmed and produced, they may be greener options than fabrics that shed plastic polymers into our water systems with every wash. And don't feel you need to shun them in second-hand form: a friend who lives in icy Vermont saves a fortune on heating by wearing her great-grandmother's fur coat indoors all winter long.

61. **The greenest outfit you'll wear is the one you already have in your wardrobe.** Stop shopping for clothes, other than undies. Buy second-hand, or keep wearing the clothes you already have. Check what clothes you might have in the mending basket, laundry basket, ironing pile or packed away in a forgotten suitcase.

62. **Get a small sewing kit together** (the little ones with pre-threaded needles provided by some hotels are a good start) and learn to mend and alter your clothes, by hand if necessary. Eight weeks of spending one hour mending each Monday morning (over coffee, with a friend) restored to me three tops, four pairs of leggings, half a dozen pairs of socks, and my favourite bra.

63. **Or find a local tailor** to repair your more expensive or durable items. I have a fleece windbreaker with zipped pockets, invaluable for walking and hiking, that's about to enter its third decade – but which has twice had to have a zip replaced.

64. **Buy not just clothing second-hand, but other home textiles as well**: quilts, curtains, carpets, even bedding and towels, if you don't mind the once-off splurge of washing them at the highest temperature setting in your washing-machine once you get them home. The exquisite crewelwork curtains I bought second-hand 20 years ago have just been repaired, along their fraying seamlines, and look brand-new again.

 One "advantage" of living in a country with a cruel and vast gap between the haves and the have-nots is that those of us who have more than we need (a weird and immoral concept, if you stop to think about it) have a nearly infinite range of options for passing on clothing – there'll be dozens of charities around the corner from you.

But in countries like Australia, where median incomes are high by world standards, and there are nanny-state restrictions on second-hand goods, tons of clothing are going into landfills. It was equally disturbing to learn that in the UK, some high-fashion cheap goods go straight from the wharf to the dump, because in the short time given to manufacture and transport, those items have already gone out of "style".

Then there was the unforeseen Marie Kondo effect in the US following her popular TV series – people enthusiastically cleared out their homes and closets, and took the contents down to charity stores. These outlets found themselves swamped with often unusable stuff, with as much as four-fifths ending up in landfills.

65. **Learn to knit and/or crochet**, if you have scraps of wool around. I am all thumbs, but even I can bodge together a scarf. Charities, crèches and schools are always looking for knitted items that can be given to those who need warm clothing during winter.

66. **A good shoe-mender is a treasure**. Resole your favourite boots regularly, and get back to the old-fashioned habit of polishing shoes to keep them looking new and in good condition for longer.

67. **Wedding dresses**: there are quite a few options. You can repurpose: one friend dyed her mother's timeless but slightly yellowed lace wedding dress and veil by dunking them in a bath of cold tea. Everything turned a delicate pinkish ivory, and she looked lovely on the day. Or give your dress away to another bride (easier if you've been through a messy divorce). If you're sentimentally attached to your dress, lend it out. This can tug at the heartstrings, especially if it's a family heirloom, but be honest: why are you keeping your mother's meringue with an ancient mayonnaise stain on the bodice? (See p. 145 for an especially moving way to recycle your wedding dress.)

68. Matric dances and similar events are sinkholes of expense, for outfits that are rarely, if ever, worn again. It's tempting to recommend that all schools should emulate the one whose principal insisted that his pupils wear school uniform to their matric dance. But this may seem cruelly austere, ironically, often to young people from poor families, who rarely get an opportunity to step out in glamorous clothing and accessories. And the importance of one magical evening can't be discounted. So **find out if there's a charity nearby that lends out clothing, shoes and accessories to young people for matric dances and similar events**, and donate all your evening gear (including bridesmaid's dresses and similar) that you are never going to fit into or wear again.

69. Organisations like these also often lend out suits and professional outfits to people going for job interviews, so these are good places to donate these items as well. **Suits and formal shoes for young men are always needed.**

70. For really dramatic clothing that today's teens might spurn or snort at (batwinged capes, feather boas, puffball skirts, etc.), **find out if there is a nearby ballet school or theatre company that might like to use them as costumes.**

71. **Join or form a second-hand clothing co-operative that does clothing swops.** I've belonged to a women's one for nearly 30 years. We meet in someone's home, bring our unwanted clothes, a plate of eats, and wander around in our undies trying each other's things on.

72. You'll encounter finger-waggers who claim the wealthy shouldn't buy second-hand clothes because they're muscling in on the territory of those who can't afford to buy new. Use your common sense – you shouldn't be buying a top for a few bucks from a charity shop that serves a poor area (or is located close to a public transport hub) unless dire financial necessity dictates. **Vintage shops are an excellent option if you're middle class.**

HOME AND FAMILY

This is the one area where we needn't feel helpless: **we can take charge of the environmental footprint of our own homes** with relatively little adaptation.

73. **Use what you already have in your home, which means maintaining things**: cleaning filters, sharpening knives, emptying the crumbs out the toaster, keeping your equipment and furniture in good nick.

74. Repairing things is all very well, but one problem, especially with electronic goods, is that the cost of the part/repair is often significant enough that we think we might as well replace the whole thing. Yet **a good handyperson can often cobble together a solution**, or fix our cellphone or vacuum-cleaner simply by servicing/cleaning it. There's an encouraging rise in this kind of job and skill in the UK at present, where repair shops are keeping tons of otherwise defunct goods out of landfills.

75. **Re-upholster rather than replace your sofas, chairs and cushions** (will someone please explain why home décor shops suddenly exploded with cushions a few years back?).

76. **Places that can use your battered old furniture**: shelters for women and children fleeing domestic violence, refugee and homeless shelters, children's homes. Crèches and educare centres are often desperate for carpets and rugs (the littlies sit on bare floors otherwise), as well as low tables, shelves, toys and stationery.

77. **Larger furniture items and major appliances that are broken or too beaten up to donate**: check if there are any skills-training workshops nearby (where folk are learning electrical repairs, upholstery, carpentry, etc.) that would be happy to receive these. There may well be local organisations (either recycling or skills-training NPOs) that will collect, either for free or for a small fee.

78. Investigate your local dump, especially if it's close by. Sometimes these have a drop-off point for bigger household items that you're replacing, but which are still functional. Depending on what systems are in place, people are often able to collect these goods for re-use or repair.

Pets: I have few qualms telling people the single greenest thing they can do is not to have children (unless they adopt), but heaven help the rigid green bean who tells me we shouldn't have pets. Domestic animals offer enormous companionship, comfort and pleasure to our lives, and teach children compassion and responsibility. People with pets, especially those with dogs that need walking, live longer and enjoy a better quality of life (ask any actuary). Domestic animals are here on the planet with us, so it's no good pretending they're not.

However, the greenest thing we can do is to spay and neuter them. There is no truth to the myth that female cats "need to have at least one litter". Animal shelters are bursting at the seams with cats and dogs in desperate need of homes; do not allow your animals to add to this burden.

Adopt, don't buy or breed. Kittens and puppies are adorable, but there's nothing like the dignity and loyalty of an older animal. Talk to your local shelter – they struggle to rehome more mature animals.

79. **Draw up a "banned list" for your home, in which your family agrees to bar certain unnecessary products** from the home. These could include fabric softener (totally unnecessary, especially if you line-dry your laundry – replace with a splash of spirit vinegar, which also cleans your machine); coffee pods; Styrofoam containers; bottled water, and more. (If you hate the taste of tap water, that's why water filters exist – if you're carrying around a bottle of water you've bought from a supermarket, you can just as easily carry your own re-usable, refillable bottle of water from home.)

80. My big waste-wise Achilles heel is the vast range of cleaning products under my sink. **Almost all detergents can be replaced with bicarb and spirit vinegar.** A *Guardian* journalist tested the claim that all household cleansers can be replaced with these two cheap, biodegradable options plus Castile soap (you can add borax, salt, washing soda and lemon juice if you want to be fancy), and found it to be true. It seems that specialist cleaning fluids (including the green products on which I've spent a fortune in my lifetime, and which still present containers in need of recycling) are yet another enormous marketing con. We truly don't need them. Once again, you can google "how to clean [anything, from your wooden floors to a silver teapot]" and you'll find a cheap and green answer (I was tickled to discover that wood can be cleaned with "salad dressing" – i.e., a mix of oil and vinegar.)

This great idea for dealing with the pungent smell of vinegar comes from the writer Christine Coates: buy five-litre bottles of spirit vinegar, decant into smaller bottles, insert lavender stalks/flowers or citrus peel and stand in the sun for a few days. The vinegar turns a pretty colour and smells delicious. Use it to clean showers, tiles, kitchen surfaces, glass, mirrors. If there's crusted or baked-on dirt, sprinkle on bicarb as well and use a little elbow grease.

I spilled a tray of gravy and fat all over the oven, splattering the sides and creating an oily charcoal puddle on the bottom. I threw a cup of bicarb at the problem, followed it with a half a cup of hot water, then left everything to stand for 24 hours, whereupon it all lifted off as smooth as silk. I wiped first with paper towels, then re-usable cloths – no scrubbing or rubbing needed. It's the cleanest my oven has ever been.

81. Laundry: apart from underwear and any clothing in which we exercise, or do manual or dirty labour (mechanics' overalls, nursing uniform, etc.), the test for washing a garment is: **it has to be visibly dirty (ring around the collar, spills down the front) or smelly before it goes in the laundry basket**. Change out of any smart or formal clothes (including uniforms) as soon as you get home, and hang them up to air. If you've been somewhere that has permeated your outfit with an unwanted smell, hang it on the line, spritz lightly with water (into which you've put a spoon of scented or apple-cider vinegar), and let it air. And protect your clothes – wear an apron (I have a wipe-down one) when cooking, and tuck a napkin into your collar when eating something gloriously messy.

82. **Poisons are literally poisonous**. Ban from your home, immediately. There is no safe way to use or dispose of these. Rather choose repellent devices or products, if you have insect, rodent or mole problems.

 **Researching the safest ways to discourage every imaginable bug or "pest" both indoors and outdoors is a rather lovely rabbit hole, with hundreds of tips for eliminating poisons and insecticides from our environment. A mere handful here: food-grade diatomaceous earth is an excellent deterrent for ants**

and cockroaches; scented plant oils, and herbs and spices such as ground mint, cloves, cinnamon and chillies, are some of the pleasanter ways of discouraging ants and flies. Mosquitoes dislike citronella oil and candles, but I find crushed lemongrass stalks even more effective, especially applied to the skin. Rubbing tea-tree or eucalyptus oil on light fittings helps discourage flies, as does my habit of giving spiders and their webs sanctuary – or, like my mama, you can opt for a fly-swatter.

Outside, ladybirds will eat your aphids; you can put up an owl-box to attract a flying rat-eater, and much more. You can also distract and reduce garden pests by interplanting and companion planting – mixing your veggies up (planting carrots and onions together, for instance), planting strong-scented herbs, chives, nasturtiums and marigolds. Earn double points by recycling your old CDs into a garden mobile that discourages birds and squirrels from raiding your fruit trees, while your children can have fun creating a scarecrow from sewing scraps.

HOW TO HAVE A WASTE-LESS BATHROOM

Everything said in *101 Water Wise Ways* applies!

83. Shower-caps: pack yours when travelling so you don't have to use the disposable one in the hotel. I haven't been able to come up with a non-plastic alternative, but I **use shower-caps until the elastic perishes**, after which they go into my travel bag to wrap around shoes when packing them in luggage.

84. **Ditch the disposable razors** – never was a plastic gadget so inaccurately named. There is no safe and green way to get rid of them. Use good old-fashioned safety razors instead, and dispose

of the blades the same way you would needle sharps. Or stop shaving: grow a beard, wax, laser your armpits (not nearly as expensive and painful as you might think) or just go natural.

85. Not only can you now **buy bamboo toothbrushes** (which cost no more than plastic ones, to my surprise), I once came across a craft collective in Zimbabwe that turned old plastic toothbrushes into crochet hooks.

86. **Toothpaste**: as with so many waste-waste options, you have two choices. You can find something clever but expensive via the internet (one company makes unwrapped pellets of paste that come in a glass jar). Or you make your own, once again for next to nothing (see pp. 51 and 86).

87. **Cotton earbuds**: a friend who windsurfs says she sees way too many of them in the water: "It's astonishing how such a tiny thing can mar an entire stretch of beach." The biodegradable kind should definitely go on your shopping list. My tip for disposing of my remaining regular cotton buds (I bought a jumbo pack years ago) isn't going to stop the planet burning, but people really like it: I snip or strip the ends into my burn bin, and chuck the remaining plastic sticks into my ecobricks. Once again, best to use fewer of them: use washable make-up brushes and sponges instead.

88. **Lose the wet wipes and cotton puffs** for cleansing the skin. Use washable flannel facecloths, like your granny did (and her skin was flawless, right?). If you must use wet wipes, make your own, or choose biodegradable ones. Never flush them (the Thames in London has a carpet of them along the bottom). I wash the non-biodegradable kinds and use them as household wipes, strainers, etc. Friends with babies tell me washable cloth wipes are far more effective than baby wipes; once again, you could also make biodegradable baby wipes.

89. **Soap and shampoo bars are now available in re-usable tins**, rather than plastic bottles, and the reports coming in are mostly good. They're not cheap, but are apparently long-lasting.

90. We'll use less of ALL this stuff if we **stop buying into the propaganda that insists we constantly wash our bodies, faces and hair**. One reason we need so many moisturisers and lotions is because we're constantly stripping our skin of its own protective oils and serums though excessive washing – once again a post-World War II phenomenon. (Since I stopped showering/washing my hair as a matter of daily routine, I've been staggered by the improvement in my overall skin and hair health.)

91. Let's face it (ha), the beauty industry, which has wrapped its tentacles around all genders in the last few decades, is a snake-oil business that flogs mostly utterly needless products for astoundingly presumptuous prices. This industry generates an excessive amount of waste. Think of all the fussy "pretty" packaging: those tiny pots, lipstick cases, plastic shampoo containers, and more.

    To tackle this, be like my clever and beautiful writer/journalist friend, Kate Sidley: **go through your bathroom cupboard and make-up box and use up absolutely everything in it before buying anything new**. Cut open those tiny expensive tubes and scrape out the contents. Same with the samples you get in magazines. If elegant local actress Grethe Fox does this, so can you.

92. When I reach **the end of a lipstick** (I hold no truck with This Will Make You Forever Young Yeah Right moisturisers, but I dearly love make-up), I scrape out the bit left behind into a special pot, add a drop of almond or coconut oil, mix, and apply with a lip brush. Because this gets added to regularly, the colour is always changing, which is fun.

93. **Make your own moisturising creams and lotions**. Quite a few people are trying this, to reduce waste, save costs and avoid slathering chemicals on their skin. The internet has a deluge of videos showing you how to do so easily, cheaply and safely. Interestingly, friends who're experimenting with this say the most costly ingredients are the pure scented oils – which aren't actually needed, and which can be replaced with lavender and herbs.

94. Note that **you can also create your own make-up**. This is beyond the ambit of this book, but YouTube, Instagram, Pinterest and a thousand green beauty blogs will tell you how, in exhaustive detail.

95. Hotels and guesthouses are already addressing the problem of the sea of **little plastic shampoo, conditioner and shower gel bottles**. Trouble is, when they replace them with big bottles to be re-used by multiple guests, they have to bolt them to the shower walls to stop folk swanning off with them. Still, that's the way to go. Meanwhile, collect those miniature bottles and soaps and donate to organisations like Rape Crisis, who put them in comfort packs to give to children who've suffered unspeakable violation.

96. **Some things are very tricky to dispose of safely**. Certain pharmaceutical and medical waste has to be disposed of professionally: used needles and other sharps, blood bags. Ask your doctor or pharmacist how to proceed. Plastic syringes can be taken apart and their component bits packed into ecobricks. Never throw away expired drugs (most especially not antibiotics or hormones), or even worse, flush them down the toilet: ask your chemist to dispose of them for you, or take them to a hospital for incineration.

97. **Periods**: there is no getting away from the fact that these are a messy business. Apart from some villages in northern Kenya, where women use dried cow dung as pads, and then bury these, there is no waste-free way to menstruate. You will need either to burn or throw away disposable pads, wash re-usable pads or period panties, or use running water to rinse mooncups and sponges. The latter two options are the greenest option, with re-usable pads maybe the best for those in water-scarce communities.

98. **Never flush used condoms**. Researching green methods of disposing of condoms and sex toys was amusing, but not in the end very enlightening. It seems these will indeed have to go out with the garbage.

99. Here's a final bathroom, beauty-and-waste-related thought: Julia Roberts was recently asked for her single most NB beauty tip. Here it comes, from one of the most iconic and bankable faces in the world: LOOK AFTER YOUR TEETH. The best part? **She doesn't use toothpaste. She brushes with bicarb. Be more like Julia.** (See p. 51 for a basic toothpaste recipe.)

Certain pharmaceutical
and medical waste
has to be disposed of
professionally – ask your
doctor or pharmacist how
to proceed.

FOOD

Food waste hits a nerve like no other. For years, I wrote charity appeal letters for holiday/Christmas food parcels for vulnerable families, invalids and pensioners. Pleading for donations so that needy folk could get such luxuries as cooking oil, rice, maize-meal, baked beans, teabags and a whole tin of jam at the same time as the supermarkets were loading their shelves with pistachio-brandy mince pies always made my head spin. And it means that red spots dance in front of my eyes when I see people throwing food away.

When did we get so blasé about wasting food? Why has it become ethically normative to ask people often earning minimum wages, who have hungry children at home, to prepare us luxury meals which we then expect them to scrape into the bin after we've taken a few bites? Most especially, why do folk let their children do this? I've lost track of how often I've seen tweens slurp down most of a milkshake and then take one listless nibble of their burger and chips before pushing their plate away.

I am at best what a friend calls a demi-vegetarian, but every time I see people chucking away meat, I have to restrain myself. "An animal DIED so that you could have it lying on your plate," I want to snap. "Could you at least show a little respect?"

It's become hugely politically incorrect to urge people to finish what's on their plates, so here's a new rule: **don't put it on your plate unless you want it all**. Think of it this way: your host or family member has made a delicious meal. You dish up, then ceremoniously scrape some of it into the trash before tucking in. Breathtakingly rude as well as insanely wasteful? How is this different from doing it at the end of a meal?

Worse, having extended our throwaway culture to food, the middle classes are no longer taught how to **stretch food, use it thriftily, and work wonders with leftovers**. My parents' generation was excellent at this, because they grew up during or right after the deprivations of World War II. Food was sometimes scarce, often sparse, and always seasonal – people cooked what was available, and every bite counted. But this takes a little skill (and a lot of common sense), and that skill has drained away with frightening speed in the last few decades. We may be addicted to TV cooking shows, but we no longer have any idea what to do with a glut of apples, or how to give leftover rice new life.

When I was 17, a change of schools meant I had to study Domestic Science for the first time. Our matric textbook was a template for what apartheid called "Christian National Education" (it assumed that only women cooked, we were all white, and we all had domestic workers – referred to as "servants"). There were chapters on how to cater for "ladies' teas" and children's parties (including tricky stuff like éclairs and Turkish delight). The pièce de résistance was the making of our own wedding cakes, right down to the marzipan and royal icing. "But this is useless," I thought. "Where's the section on how to stretch a pound of mince and a celery stalk into supper for a family of six?" I had to work it out myself: oats, grated carrot and lots of chopped onion. It took a few more years before I discovered Indian cooking (and shops) and the glory of red lentils and proper spices.

But while it takes a bit of planning and practice, we can not only curb wasting food, but we can make it go further. This requires regular investigation of the fridge, the freezer (if you have one), and the pantry. You have to think 24 hours ahead, and plan menus. The following tips will help, but you'll need to **develop your own food hacks**, depending on what you and your family eat – which is determined by culture, religion, budget, availability, ethical stance and much more.

100. Here's a good start: **say grace before a meal**. Yes, even if you're a hard-core atheist. Stop and THINK before you pick up your fork. Consider all the elements that went into making what's on your plate, that everyday magic of air, water, soil, seeds, crops, animals, labour, loving hands and care. Breathe. Enjoy the aromas. And give thanks. It will make us all more mindful and thoughtful eaters.

101. The opposite of wasting – "recycling" food and water via seeds and soil – is one of the most basic and necessary human activities. And almost everyone can take part: a flat-dwelling friend who poured all her washing-up water on her pot-plants soon found herself harvesting three different varieties of home-grown tomatoes and chillies. Even if it's just a squash plant on the compost heap or a herb in a pot, **growing food is good for us and the planet**. If you live in a flat or a crowded township, investigate the possibility of community gardens or an option similar to the UK's allotment system.

 It's all very well encouraging folk to plant and grow their own food, but water is increasingly a challenge. Fortunately, many veggies thrive on washing-up water. Install a water filter (it's easy to build your own – see *101 Water Wise Ways* or the blessed internet) in your veg patch. One friend solved the problem of growing veggies in a drought by planting fruit trees to create shade. This may seem counterintuitive, but it worked. Food gardening guru Jane Griffiths also works on a "jungle garden" system, where more tender plants shelter under more robust ones. I've found this with my feral butternut plants; even in the hot, arid summers of the Cape, they shade the more delicate and slow-growing stuff.

102. The real expert on how to use your leftovers and fridge contents in the most economical but deliciously epicurean ways is my friend, the writer Megan Kerr. It's from her that I **learned to keep my fridge organised.** This helps prevent that infuriating but familiar experience of finding something mutating into a new life-form while lurking behind a jar of olives. Just making sure that the tallest things stand at the back, with the rest of the contents ranked by height, helps. Every other day, open all the drawers/flaps to remind yourself of what needs using up.

103. It's also from Megan that **I've learned the value of lists: not just shopping lists, but inventories**: scribbled lists of what's in the fridge or pantry that needs using up. Crossing those items off as they get turned into meals is most satisfactory, and then you simply transfer them to your shopping list.

104. I also learned from my parents, who were very good at inventive combinations of leftovers. They taught me the basics: **runny or soggy leftovers** (sauces, gravies, curries, cooked soft veg like cabbage, spinach, gem squash, marrows, mashed potatoes, carrots) can be whizzed into soup: fry an onion, toss in all the leftovers, add stock and maybe half a tin of chopped tomatoes, lots of herbs, garlic when Papa isn't looking, and blend. A stick blender is useful, but a fork and a strong arm will do the job.

105. **More "intact" food** (bits of chicken, sausages, cooked peas, beans, corn – along with cooked butternut, pumpkin, broccoli and cauliflower if not too soft, in which case, see soup above) can be sliced into salads, turned into sandwich fillings or (when all else fails) eaten cold with a dollop of mayonnaise. (Hint: if you roast your veggies, they make wonderful salad ingredients the next day.) To keep things interesting and healthy, try to put at least one fresh thing on the table at each meal.

106. The holy trinity, both for **re-inventing leftovers and livening up carbs and legumes**: onion, garlic, tomatoes (tinned or paste). I'd add a fourth: chillies. (And a handful of fresh herbs from your windowsill pots: mint, rosemary, basil, parsley, thyme, dhania/coriander, wild rocket, garlic chives, lovage.) Millions of families do this routinely to stretch from payday to payday.

107. Here are some **more leftover ideas**:

→ Bits of hardening cheese can be grated, then frozen.

→ Stale bread can be toasted, whirred into breadcrumbs (good for thickening soups and sauces) or turned into croutons or melba toast. I've turned hot cross buns into biscotti by thinly slicing and drying out in a low oven.

→ Elderly tomatoes can be roughly chopped and gently fried with lots of garlic and basil – they turn into a chunky sauce that can be frozen just about forever.

→ If you're not confident about making jam (too much sugar, too much fussing over pectin and jelling), nearly all fruit can easily be turned into chutney or sauces for either sweet or savoury dishes. Wrinkly apples can either be turned into chutney or simmered with cinnamon, ginger and a spoonful of honey or brown sugar – the resulting sauce can be spooned onto cereals, stirred into yoghurt, or eaten with pork.

→ Berries and tropical fruits like paw-paw and mangoes can be blended with yoghurt or milk, as for smoothies, and then frozen. If you whir them up again before they've completely defrosted, you get rather nice slushies. Ripe bananas can be peeled and frozen, then whizzed straight into smoothies.

→ Buy only small amounts of food like lettuce and cucumber that go off quickly. This is another reason why growing your own greens is a great idea – your veg bed is actually an outdoor pantry in which everything is always fresh.

108. As with many things, Google is your friend. If you have an unusual array of leftovers or pantry items, you can run them all into the search bar, and then add "recipe" – and see what comes up. This can be quite an adventure.

All genders need to do this work (and to know how to do it). We've been hearing about how women are saddled with what's known as "emotional labour" and the "mental load" even in households where domestic chores are supposedly shared. Maybe one of the factors contributing to food waste is that women are fed up being the ones who have to remember to defrost the bolognaise sauce that's been in the freezer for two months, and then check that there's spaghetti to go with it.

109. Possibly the most waste-wise change we can make concerning our food is to **become … not a vegetarian (see overleaf), but a locavore**. One of the hidden wastages surrounding food is the energy cost of the miles it travels to reach us ("food miles"). This is why the closer to home our food is, the less it costs the planet. This is also why we should eat food in season: it's fresher, tastier, and hasn't had to be imported (often via plane). Another troubling factor about imported food is that it often has to meet quality standards that have nothing to do with nutrition and everything to do with appearance: which means an enormous amount is wasted even before it reaches us.

This is not the place for a debate of the ethics of eating flesh. However, our transformation of animal husbandry into a massive and inhumane industry, and our rapacious stripping of the seas of their edible contents, is proving disastrous for every living thing involved, including our short-sighted selves.

From a green perspective, humans need to eat less meat. But from a strictly environmental perspective, vegan and even vegetarian diets are not necessarily good for the planet in arid and semi-arid regions. Ruminants occupy a vital stage in the food chain between plants and humans, because they are able to digest grass and other tough fibrous plants, and convert these to protein. Humans, let loose on a pasture of waving grasses and no other food sources, would starve. Add a pig, sheep, goat or a few chickens into this scenario, however, and we could live quite well.

Deer, free-ranging cattle and other grazing animals can, by nibbling down more invasive species of grass, and also manuring pastures, increase the biodiversity of a landscape, and its capacity for sustenance.

Obviously this does NOT apply to factory-farming and feedlots, which gobble up grains that could feed humans directly, generate vast amounts of slurry and methane – a particularly dangerous greenhouse gas – and are generally places of suffering so heinous they do not bear contemplation.

One resolution you could make: not to eat misery meat (which rules out much of the junk meat sold by the ubiquitous fast-food chains). Meat should be eaten sparingly, from nose to tail, and should come from humanely farmed sources. The more we push for this, the more affordable it will become; although frankly, if we're going to eat meat, it should be costly to reflect the reality of its journey to our plate.

110. **Speaking of ethical eating, there's one product we**
should **be boycotting – palm oil**. It has great benefits for
the food industry, as it is stable, palatable and healthier than
some oils used in commercial food preparation. Unfortunately,
it needs to be grown in tropical zones, and in Indonesia,
indigenous forests are being clear-cut to make room for palm
plantations. This deforestation has led to habitat loss for
endangered species that include the orangutan. As discussed
on p. 134, cutting down established and indigenous forests
in a time of accelerating climate change is the equivalent of
cutting out bits of our lungs.

**Journalist Nechama Brodie has prepared a list of products
for sale in South Africa (mostly food, but some toiletries) that
contain palm oil (see 'Resources' on p. 149) – print it out and
take it shopping with you. Note that because of international
pressure, marketing boards are trying to establish sources of
palm oil that do not have jackbooted environmental footprints,
and it's likely that in future we'll be able to buy the equivalent
of certified "fairtrade" palm oil. Until then, give products made
with it a miss.**

111. **Ditch the snacks.** Snacking (other than on fruit) was invented
by advertising and marketing agencies after World War II.
Worse, the calibre of snack food ranges from blah (do corn
chips really excite you?) to downright unhealthy. The notion
of carrying around packets of processed foods to munch on
throughout the day is relatively new, and largely unnecessary.

112. Many Europeans shop at markets first thing in the morning,
armed with string and cloth bags, to ensure that the food they
eat is as fresh as possible. We can take a leaf from their book
and **return to "old-fashioned" shopping habits: buying
from the butcher, fishmonger and baker.**

113. It is also possible to **take containers to the butchery in supermarkets**, order your cut of meat, and have it packed into your own containers. Likewise, take (scrupulously clean) containers to the fish counter, and ask the staff not just to fillet your fish, but to give you the skin, guts and bones to take home in a separate Tupperware. Bury these in your veg garden: an ancient trick for producing magnificent tomatoes.

114. Although some people are still too embarrassed to **ask for a doggie bag** or put their restaurant leftovers into a Tupperware, this is becoming not just acceptable but encouraged. Tupperware is a great solution to the problem of "portion distortion" in restaurants, imported from the US. It's also better to take your own containers than to use those supplied by restaurants, many of which still pack food in polystyrene and other unrecyclable containers. Thumbs up to those restaurants that supply biodegradable takeaway containers – but re-usable is best.

CELEBRATIONS AND FESTIVALS

There's not a human culture or society since the beginning of time that hasn't celebrated happy (or even sorrowful) occasions with banquets, fermented liquids, roaring fires, colourful costumes and showers of flower petals. Celebrate life and its significant moments: it's a wonderful, comforting and joyous thing to do. But our special events and calendar moments have become orgies of waste-generating and wasteful consumption. **We need to rethink the way we celebrate.**

It *is* completely possible to have green Christmases, religious festivals, Halloweens, weddings, birthday and anniversary parties, even funerals.

I'd be grateful for tips on green ways to celebrate important festivals – Ramadan, Diwali, Passover, Hanukkah and others – across a wider range of religions. Please send these to me via www.helenmoffett.com/green-hat so that they can be included in future editions of this book.

115. **Children's birthday parties**: in the past few decades, these have turned into three-ringed circuses generating piles of waste: single-use balloons and streamers, party favours, themed napkins, goodie bags, two streams of catering (children and adults), gift-wrapping and more. Part of the problem with countering this is the element of competition – all the "other" children and their parents are doing this. It can be hard digging in your heels in the face of pleading children, so make it a point of pride to host alternative parties, where the food is home-made, adults are expected to treat the event as a potluck (or at least to bring a bottle), and instructions on waste-wise gift-giving and wrapping are issued to all parents of invited children.

116. This applies to all parties and events like weddings. There's no need to exclude festive elements, but don't create piles of rubbish that need to be scooped into garbage bags at the end of the day. Rather **use décor that can enjoy another**

outing: fabric, ribbons, colourful drawings, and gift-wrapping that can be re-used. A friend sews strings of re-usable bunting for special events. Your rule of thumb décor-wise should be first to aim for stuff that can be re-used, then recycled or composted (so you could festoon everything in ivy or flowers, for example).

117. **The same goes for corporate and branded events**: no more "gag" gifts, and if you must dole out mementoes, make sure they're useful and re-usable.

118. **Ban balloons.** There is no safe way to dispose of them; they fly away and all too often end up in the ocean, choking some poor sea creature. Fly kites instead.

119. The Black Christmases of the 1980s (boycotting, for political reasons, everything except the four Fs: family, friends, faith and food) taught many that **the "holiday" season does not have to be a frenzy of shopping, presents, decorations, cards, malls, with too much alcohol sloshing around**, contributing to Russian roulette on the roads and domestic mayhem. No one wants to be a Christmas Grinch, but there are kinder, gentler and thriftier ways of celebrating – whether wrapping presents in your children's drawings, making gifts (time-consuming but satisfying), or donating the gift budget to charity.

120. **Gift-giving**:
   → It can be fun matching people to the perfect **charity projects**: donate to an animal shelter or pay for a spay for your dog-loving aunt; plant trees or give to food garden projects for the gardening enthusiast; support child literary projects in honour of your booky pals – the list is endless. Google and even social media are great helps in finding perfect projects in your own backyard.

→ At the end of the year, instead of presents for distant cousins, why not get **grocery vouchers for the service staff** (wait-staff, porters, till-packers, car and security guards, cleaners, petrol-station attendants, shampoo personnel and more) who've made your life a bit easier this year?

→ Consider giving **green gifts**: bamboo travel mugs, re-usable shopping bags, solar torches – any green gift catalogue will have hundreds of ideas. Or gifts that exist only in the ether: subscriptions to online magazines and newspapers, for instance.

→ **Food and drink** are always welcome as gifts – just make sure they're appropriate (no biltong for your vegan colleague, wine for your devout Muslim neighbour, or sweets for your diabetic aunt). This alone means stopping to think about what the recipient might appreciate and enjoy – which is the point.

→ Give gifts on the clear understanding that the recipient is welcome to pass them on: I love print books, so I will often buy one for a fellow book enthusiast with the rider that they're free to either keep it or give to someone who will enjoy it, who will in turn **pass it on to someone else or donate it to a library**, and so on.

→ Keep and **re-use wrapping paper**. Or wrap gifts using your children's artwork, as suggested earlier. Another option is to use gift bags, and to keep re-using them. They're also good for donating to organisations that give gift bags or hampers to those in need.

→ **Make cards** (repurpose a colourful postcard or family photo) or buy charity ones. Or ask your children to make them with craft supplies or their own art.

→ **Valentine's Day**: The commercial festival of Valentine's Day has created a sea of red paper, tinsel, yet more pink plastic puffery and mediocre chocolate rattling around in way too much packaging. Unless you have an organic pick-your-own rose farm on your doorstep (I do), the traditional red roses need to go. If you must buy cut flowers, go for indigenous and local, not blooms that have been whizzed around the country or the globe in an oil-slurping aeroplane. In fact, **replace cut flowers with a plant**. A colourful pot plant can be just as beautiful as a bouquet, and even nicer is an edible plant, or something quirky, like a succulent.

→ Substitute heavily packaged and individually wrapped chocolates with **home-made sweets**. The possibilities are multiple: heart-shaped biscuits, delicious date-coconut-nut truffles, home-made peanut brittle, and a thousand variations on chocolate brownies and muffins. What's nice about this kind of V-day gesture is that you'll be making entire batches, so there's a lot more love to go around – you can show up at your child's school, your sewing collective, your workshop, or your book club with cupcakes for your colleagues, children's teachers, friends and even your enemies. Of which you will promptly have less.

→ Yes, a special meal in a restaurant is nice. And it's completely possible to have a waste-wise evening out (see *101 Water Wise Ways* for how cafés and restaurants can make a green difference). But consider whipping up **a special meal at home** and eating it by candlelight.

121. Lent and Easter:

→ For those who mark this time of the Christian year, my Quaker friend Sue Mottram suggests that instead of giving up chocolate or coffee, rather put a household item or piece of clothing in a box for each of the 40 days of Lent. Come Easter, donate this box to a charity or shelter for refugees or homeless people.

→ If living plastic-free is new to you, try giving up plastic, or at least single-use plastic, for Lent.

→ And everything said above about Valentine chocolate applies to Easter as well.

**Replace cut flowers
with a plant.**

OUT AND ABOUT IN THE WORLD

In terms of waste-less ways, **we have less control when in public spaces** and at work. If you practise stringently green habits at home, it can come as a shock to see people around you drinking from plastic bottles and takeaway cups, or worse, littering. But there are some steps you can take.

122. **Don't chuck recyclable litter into a bin unless you know it will indeed be recycled** – rather take your garbage home with you.

123. **Challenge litterbugs**, especially those who drop fast-food packaging in the street. One of the reasons floods did so much damage in Durban in 2019 was that storm-water drains were blocked by rubbish consisting mostly of fast-food containers. A feisty Caribbean colleague out on a visit tore a strip off a burly taxi-driver who threw away a soft-drink can; she shamed him into picking it up. (His excuse at first: he was "creating employment".)

124. Speaking of shaming, one tactic proposed by green activists is to **photograph litter that has visible corporate or product branding**, and then to post pictures to those companies' social media pages. This is a form of pressure spoken about on p. 17 – passing the waste buck back to big corporates, who need to take responsibility for the (over)packaging they produce.

125. This really involves taking one for the team, but **pick up litter in public areas** (wear stout gloves). One very bleak day, I was inspired by a woman on my local beach who was picking up every piece of washed-up plastic she came across, filling a huge sack in the process. Your neighbourhood might well have communal litter-collection activities and walks. After a devastating fire swept through the mountains surrounding my home, locals seized the opportunity to pick up all the glass bottles tossed into the bushes and revealed by the

fire. There are several lessons to be learned here: collective activity is powerful; pay attention to your own backyard; nearly every environmental challenge (fire, in this case) offers an opportunity for some kind of regeneration.

126. **Pack a waste-wise basket or bag**, and get into the habit of taking it with you everywhere. This might contain your travel mug, water bottle, a cloth napkin, chopsticks and even ice in a thermos.

127. **Take the stairs instead of the lift** – the latter are great electricity guzzlers. If it's a matter of a few flights, and you're able-bodied, look for the stairs.

128. **Stop flying around the country and indeed the globe** for meetings, work junkets and training days, etc. THIS IS WHAT SKYPE IS FOR. International conferences and their organisers need to think hard about online means of gathering to exchange ideas and research. I was impressed when the keynote speaker at an environmental conference in South Africa presented his paper – from New York – via Skype. (See also Tip 142.)

129. **Ban bottled water at meetings**. Set out jugs of tap water and glasses.

130. Likewise, **say no to disposable catering equipment**, UNLESS this is compostable. And then make sure it is in fact composted.

131. It's a tiny thing, but if you do internet banking on your laptop or phone, **you need never print out a balance slip when drawing cash at an ATM**.

132. If you have an internet connection, unless your accountant insists on paper, **ask to receive all your accounts, bills and statements electronically**.

133. **Making use of the green spaces close to you is a wonderful way of spending quality time with family and friends**. You'll be doing your children a power of good, giving them space to run and play, the opportunity to learn to respect and identify with nature, and to help take care of it as they grow older.

    In the UK, the National Trust and similar organisations that operate stately homes, gardens, parks and moors, tailor inexpensive excursions to families so that folk who live in crammed cities can get out to enjoy green vistas and breathing spaces on the weekends – better still, they can often do so using public transport. I'd love to see more of these kinds of opportunities offered here at home, although many schools do a great job in this respect.

THE RADICAL, UNPOPULAR AND DOWNRIGHT WEIRD STUFF

Brace yourselves. Here comes **the difficult and the controversial stuff** – and I'm not (just) talking about rioting in the streets.

134. If you follow a middle-class lifestyle, **not having your own biological children is the greenest thing you'll ever do**, with 50% greater impact than any other lifestyle choices, including living off-grid and giving up car and plane travel. Yes, people find this very difficult to hear, but the evidence is unarguable.

135. **Adoption, on the other hand** is one of the most environmentally responsible choices you can make. Journalist Marianne Thamm puts it simply: "We should take responsibility for the children who are already here."

136. This one is for the blokes: the single biggest thing you can do to reduce the waste you and your potential offspring will generate in your lifetime and afterwards? **Have a vasectomy**. It's far more sensible (as well as safer, cheaper, medically much less invasive) to sterilise men than women. We're fertile for three days a month for 30 years; you're a potential bunny rabbit every single day from puberty until the grave.

137. **Trade in the gas guzzler for a smaller car**, or (if yours is a two-car family) sell one of them. Better still, get a hybrid vehicle – although very small cars with low fuel consumption sometimes beat these in the green stakes.

138. **Our attitude to money needs to change profoundly**. Remember the meme about the names we call those who hoard used teabags or newspapers, or keep 47 cats? Do this with money, however, and you make the Fortune 500 list. Yet dosh is a good ONLY if it keeps circulating in society. Hoarding money and hiding it in tax havens the way the extremely rich

(by this I mean anyone who accumulates more money than they or their families could ever possibly need in their lifetimes) often do is vile. Praising and emulating those who hoard money is obscene. And, no, billionaires do not need to set aside megatons of money for their children. Paul and Linda McCartney made their daughter Stella save up for her first car – a second-hand Beetle. And look at her now: successful and rich on her own terms.

139. **Tax the rich.** Hard. Harder. Close all loopholes and criminalise tax havens. Something I find very hard to swallow is that the amount of cash in tax havens alone could end world hunger, forgive all student debt, and save the planet. And yet few governments pursue the screamingly obvious solutions – ensuring that the super-rich pay their taxes. Billionaire investor Warren Buffett made headlines in 2013 when he pointed out that his secretary was taxed at a higher rate than he was – that because of tax breaks doled out to the super-rich, he was in fact paying probably the lowest tax rate in his entire building. You do not need me to tell you that this is immoral. As we prepared to send this manuscript to print, the news broke that Amazon, whose minimum-wage workers report repetitive-strain injuries and allegedly pee into bottles because there is no time for bathroom breaks, paid zero federal income tax on their 2018 *profit* of 11 BILLION US dollars. Once more, with feeling: Tax. The. Rich.

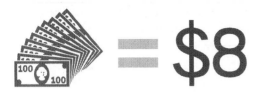 = $8

Philanthropy is sadly not a solution to proper taxation of the extremely rich. Some very rich people do indeed donate millions – but often to causes that do not advance the dignity or safety of the human race, much less the salving of the planet's wounds. Donations reflect the particular interests or political concerns of the donors rather than being spread democratically across a range of needs. In theory, if I pay ten thousand rand in tax, this money goes to all publicly funded institutions and services, even if I have no interest, for instance, in maintaining roads or mowing verges, and would rather all my taxes went towards education, libraries, and perhaps a home for elderly cats. The impersonal disbursement of most taxation systems has the benefit of being fair – unless the hands of the corrupt get involved, which is a topic for another entire book, as well as cause for epic rage.

A case that illustrates the point about both philanthropy and taxation: when Notre Dame cathedral burned in 2019, centuries of beauty and history going up in flames, three French billionaires pledged hundreds of millions for its restoration. Yet financial journalists noted that these individuals were so wealthy, the amounts they offered (which added up to almost a billion euros) were equivalent to someone who earned 50 thousand dollars a year donating eight dollars. Now imagine if those individuals were taxed at the same rates as ordinary citizens.

140. **Stop subsidising the fossil fuel industry, especially with our taxes.** This is like paying someone to push a bus full of people over a cliff.

141. Divest from fossil fuel companies. Contact your financial planner and find out where your pension is invested. Put pressure on big financial institutions to **switch to green investment plans**. This will also give alternative economic systems a boost.

142. **Cut down on travel, most especially on planes**. OK, this one hurts. My elderly parents live 1600 kilometres away from me, and the only practical way of getting to them in a hurry is to fly. But only 50 years ago, air travel was a rare and exotic luxury, or something necessitated by extremity, like war. Cricket teams setting off from Australia or South Africa to play Test matches in Britain or with each other first faced weeks at sea. I would happily travel only by boat and rail (my two favourite forms of transport) for the rest of my life, but the world is no longer shaped this way. Yet we are facing a future in which air travel may well become a luxury undertaken for humanitarian or compassionate reasons – a family wedding, a visit to a sick relative. In the meantime, although it's a far-from-perfect solution, plant a small forest every time you take a flight (some airlines make this easy for you by giving you the option of paying a "carbon tax").

143. Opt out. **Go entirely off-grid**. A few of my friends have done this; retreated to small cabins in the countryside where they're clearing alien vegetation, planting trees, replenishing soil, rehabilitating waterways, growing their own food, practising self-sufficiency. British environmentalist Mark Boyle, explaining why he has jumped off the grid, writes: "I'm now more interested in keeping the best of the old ways alive, preserving a link from our ancient past – and its crafts, perspectives, stories – into our future, so that when the industrial apparatus collapses under the weight of its own junk, these long-serving ways can point us towards the back roads home."

One of the most difficult things to shift: our understanding of what is good and evil. We need to acknowledge that wasting resources and consuming them greedily and needlessly is immoral. Yet we still see these actions as personal choices that no one has the right to dictate to us: driving a big 4x4; ordering a luxury meal in a restaurant and then sending it back to the kitchen to be thrown away; yanking out indigenous plants and replacing them with lawn or paving; chopping down mature trees to build a car park. In today's moral universe, it simply doesn't occur to us that these actions might be unethical.

Wasteful ways need to be viewed the same way as lying, cheating and stealing, because they are the same: we're lying (to ourselves and others) when we deny the scientific evidence for climate change. We're cheating our fellow global citizens of lives that will be decent, comfortable and secure; and we're stealing from our children – the air they will need to breathe and the water they will need to drink in the future.

All that said, scolding and judging are not ideal ways to bring about a revolution. Angry as I am about the disparities of income and opportunity that go hand in hand with scraping the planet bare, I am only too aware that making individuals feel guilty and ashamed is not the answer.

Debating this with a friend who has "skin in the game" (i.e. small children), we spoke about new understandings of morality that encompass a sense of collective responsibility: the labour, but also the relief, of realising that we are part of a greater whole. We need to recognise that we bear obligations not just to our families and friends, but our neighbours, fellow citizens and all living denizens of the globe.

The last 50 years have seen the rise of the "I got mine" or "I'm all right, so the hell with you" mindsets, in which we are actively discouraged from sharing, from opening up the opportunities we've enjoyed to others, jealously guarding our little patches of privilege. The truth is that understanding that we are not islands, but part of the mainland (to paraphrase the poet John Donne); that we solve problems best with the support of others; that we are team players by nature and design, is more encouraging than wringing our hands over our wicked ways.

144. Did you know **you can recycle your own body**? Here are some ways to do this (**you don't have to die first**):

→ **Give blood.** People are sometimes reluctant to donate blood because they don't think "drunk drivers and warring gangsters" deserve it (a common misconception). The truth is that nearly all donated blood goes to mothers who lose too much blood during childbirth, with the rest mostly going to surgery patients; while platelet donations go mostly to children being treated for leukaemia and other cancers.

→ **Register as an organ donor**. Hundreds of people who die in hospital each year have families who refuse the harvesting of their organs because they are unsure whether the deceased would have wanted that. Trust me, once you're dead, you no longer have any use for those corneas or kidneys. Unless religious strictures forbid you from doing so, register today, and make sure your nearest and dearest know you have done so.

→ Small but satisfying thing to do: if you have long, thick, healthy hair, consider having it cropped to **make wigs for chemotherapy patients**. A few people I know grow their hair especially for this purpose. Meanwhile, ask your hairdresser to stuff hair-sweepings into old pillowcases to donate to an animal shelter for bedding.

→ **Mortal remains**: There is almost no environmentally friendly way to dispose of a body, as anyone who reads

Patricia Cornwell or Kathy Reichs thrillers will be able to tell you (although perhaps the "sky burials" of certain cultures, in which bodies are literally fed to vultures, are an exception). Research the options (basically, various forms of burial, cremation, or donating your body to a medical school). Washington State has just become the first one in the US that permits the "composting" of bodies: you can opt to be turned into a bag of soil – but don't bank on this being available in South Africa anytime soon.

→ If you want **a green funeral**, make these wishes known and attach these details to your will. You might be happy to abandon notions of dignity (I'd like to be buried upright, in a shroud, with a tree planted on my head), but remember that while these details will be irrelevant to you after your death, they may be extremely important to members of your family and community.

What we must let go of, however, are the fancy caskets and elaborate mausoleums. I understand the need for a headstone or marker (although I like the idea of rocks and trees), but a casket that by definition lies mouldering underground is a waste in every sense of the word.

I like the US practice of interment: that the ashes following cremation are then buried, rather than scattered, in a special spot or graveyard, especially if there is a family plot – this allows the option of a commemorative plant or stone.

Washington State has just
become the first one in
the US that permits the
"composting" of bodies.

CITIZEN ACTIVISM: WORKING TOGETHER FOR CHANGE

The Rebecca Solnit quotation at the front of this book alludes to our over-reliance on a hero narrative – that some special or significant person will emerge to save the day. To save the planet, however, is going to take the power of the collective. Perhaps a downside of having so much individual choice is that we have forgotten how to work as part of citizen groups and teams. Yet, in order to create the necessary public pressure on governments (local and national), corporations, state enterprises and businesses, **we need to gather together so that our voices are heard**.

These are all the waste-wise changes we need to agitate for, but where we're unlikely to make progress if we do so as solo operators. Doing so in groups, however, helps roll the boulder uphill.

145. So to push for these changes (and save the planet), **we need to become joiners**. Churches, schools, community organisations all offer a way in. Sign up for PTAs, ratepayers' associations, and establish a green or environmental committee for every community of which you are part: residential, professional and recreational.

146. **Safe, reliable, clean public transport** is essential if we are to stop wasting both time and fossil fuels, and extracting frustration. But because it's mostly the poor who use public transport in South Africa, and because of the all-but-overt contempt the state has for its poorer citizens, our systems have almost crumbled.

     Yet this is one of the most effective ways of reducing both carbon emissions and stress. According to 2011 figures, 21% of Cape Town's emissions are produced by cars. Meanwhile, actuarial studies show that decent, functioning public transport adds years to our lifespans, while driving in rush-hour traffic for more than 60 minutes a day (in total) shaves as much as seven years off our lives. Commitment to decent, safe public transport requires other social changes as well: I used public transport all through my late teens and twenties, but finally stopped doing so (a choice not open to many South African women) because of the atmosphere of ongoing sexual harassment.

147. Alongside public transport in the form of buses and trains, **we need investment in supporting infrastructures**: innovations similar to the tuk-tuks in India that run on gas, not petrol or diesel; parkades roofed with solar panels providing electricity to the adjacent buildings; recharge stations for electric cars, and more.

148. We need to **push for far more investment and research into wind, wave and solar power options,** as well as refinements that can improve these systems and make them cheaper to install, more durable and easier to maintain.

149. We need **tax rebates and incentives for going off the electricity grid**; as in many other countries, we need systems that enable individual households to pump power back into the grid.

150. Flex your consumer muscles and **vote with your wallet**. We now have the influential tool of social media to make demands, such as insisting that supermarkets use less packaging.

151. One of the most valuable green resources you'll encounter: your library. Obviously, a shared resource (of books, in this case), as well as space to knit, do homework, read the papers, go online, do research, is good for us and the planet. But **consider other forms of libraries**: tool libraries and toy libraries are growing in popularity in countries such as Canada. These are essentially all based on the principle that we will need much less stuff if we share goods on a community basis.

152. Insist on **the "right to repair"** – that manufacturers stop sealing their products so that they cannot be repaired, or insisting that attempts to fix them will invalidate the

guarantee. Workshops that repair goods not only keep them out of landfills; Australian author Katherine Wilson found this had economic and social benefits. She quotes economist Richard Denniss: a community that repairs its goods "would employ more people, per dollar spent, than a community that instinctively disposes of them". And that's not counting the personal satisfaction gained from repairing things.

153. **Own your wild spaces. Reclaim them.** One of the surprises of travelling in Europe and North America, especially after a childhood in apartheid South Africa, in which public spaces were racially segregated, was to find parks, public gardens and other beauty spots full of people enjoying the benefits of fresh air, blooms and birdsong. Here at home, we have a new blight on our beauty spots: those visiting them are often targeted for attack (sometimes violent) by criminals. This is not the space to propose ways and means of tackling this serious problem, but one thing we can do that will make our wild and precious spaces safer is to occupy them. Thugs are (hopefully) not going to wade into crowds of picnickers or joggers.

154. Because the response to green initiatives is so often "But what about growth? What about the economy?", it is worth stopping to consider that saving the planet is going to be such a full-time and enormous task that it's going to be the huge job creator of the near future – and that will be a fine thing. **We need to think hard about what new sorts of jobs and economic models the future will hold, and then push for them.** These could involve recycling; repurposing; building different kinds of infrastructure, including green homes and office buildings; clearing alien vegetation; building and rehabilitating waterways and dams, wind farms and mills.

CAN THIS PLANET BE SAVED?

So we've adapted our lifestyles; we're using less of everything; we're Skype-ing instead of flying to meetings; we've swopped our big car for a little one. We may have reduced our footprint on the planet, but **is there more we could be doing?** Are there proactive steps we can take?

Yes! There are solutions to the parlous state of our burning planet that offer long-term hope. Science writer Leonie Joubert has already pointed out that **natural spaces and green zones** provide critical buffers or "airbags" against climate-driven disasters such as storms, cyclones, floods and fire. She explains how rehabilitating certain wetlands and vleis adjacent to some of Cape Town's poorer urban areas has helped to protect these neighbourhoods during times of storm-driven floods. Here's another small example. When wildfires swept through the southern-most tip of the Cape Peninsula a few years ago, families living in wooden houses in the direct line of the fire were evacuated, and expected their homes to burn to the ground. But the properties were surrounded by carpets of "suur vy", an indigenous succulent, and the ravaging flames simply went around them. The same was seen in the devastating fires that rampaged through three Cape coastal villages at the start of 2019: houses that had alien vegetation in their gardens burned, while those surrounded by indigenous plants were often spared.

This means that rehabilitating wetlands and grasslands, clearing alien vegetation and replacing it with indigenous plants, restoring biodiversity in terms of microbe, plant and insect life (something as simple as cultivating plants with yellow and blue flowers to attract bees) are not nice-to-haves: they soften the blows of climate chaos, and are critical to the planet's survival – and therefore our survival. These are **projects we can almost all get stuck into**, even on a tiny scale: if we plant wild rocket in our backyard, we can have salad all year round AND support local bee colonies; the entire family can go on litter-collecting walks; those of us who enjoy hiking can take part in alien-clearing "hackathons" in outdoor areas and wetlands.

155. One of the most effective things we can start doing is almost laughably simple: **plant more trees**. According to Garret Barnwell, psychologist and former president of Médecins Sans Frontières (MSF) Southern Africa, "Reforestation is the cheapest and most natural way to combat climate change." As the Chinese proverb goes: "The best time to plant a tree is 20 years ago. The second-best time is now." Better still, we can choose plants that are waterwise, indigenous and exceptionally effective at carbon uptake.

Tom Crowther, a professor at a Swiss university, heads a research team that has published the astonishing finding that we can heal the planet – by planting a trillion trees, a call that's been supported by British politician Ed Miliband and others. The research is so far mostly confined to the northern hemisphere, Brazil and Australia, but shows that the best effects will come from planting in the tropics – so it will be vital to show projections for the African continent. What's needed is to plant appropriately for climate, region and water supply, and to make best use of "waste" public land, or previously forested land. Natural savannas and grasslands should be respected and appropriately planted. Forests or shrublands need to be indigenous, and in more arid regions, water-wise.

South Africans have great hopes for the humble spekboom (Portulacaria afra), an apparently indestructible shrub-tree with round edible leaves, as it absorbs four times the usual amounts of carbon. An experimental land restoration project in the Eastern Cape, where 1 500 hectares were planted with spekboom taken from cuttings, has been hugely successful in restoring degraded land and waterways, but ecologists are pointing out that farmers are not paid for vital activities such as carbon-storing, flood prevention, or soil and biodiversity restoration.

It's clear that new forms of public-private funding will have to develop around activities that restore the environment – as well as new commercial models. The bank that provided the loan for the wine farm that floated solar panels across their dams noted this as well: that financial and funding models for agriculture and green restoration are going to have to move swiftly into the future.

The tip here? Go plant a spekboom. Or two, or three, or a thousand.

156. Trees, plants and soil all have carbon-sequestering properties – they can actually draw down ("sink") carbon from the atmosphere like sponges. This is why it is such a grave offence against the planet to chop down existing and indigenous trees, especially those in tropical regions (clear-cutting Amazonian forest growth and forests in Indonesia to create pastures for beef or palm-oil plantations is devastating not just to the rare species they house, but for us – those are planetary lungs we're slashing and burning). I'd like to see **legislative overhaul that makes it an offence to cut down established trees or remove indigenous growth**, even on private property.

157. We can also **plant for future food security**: monoculture and standardised crops have edged out local and indigenous food plants, but finding these, growing them, and sharing their seeds is an important proactive step many can take. These crops often draw only gently from the soil (or even replenish it), are suited to the immediate micro-climate (so need less water, feeding and protection from insects), and are more resistant to local bugs and diseases.

A South African example: former businesswoman Siphiwe Sithole is growing indigenous bambara (jugo) beans on her

Gauteng farm not just because they're nutritionally a complete food (and delicious – with a slightly nutty flavour), but because they fix essential nitrogen in the soil, while the leaves and pods provide animal fodder and mulch.

Here's the kind of win-win, low-tech, income-generating scheme we need: in East Africa, small farmers who struggle with elephants trampling and eating their subsistence crops are fencing their fields with beehives. Elephants give these a wide berth; the farmers can grow their crops in peace, and they have the bonus of honey to consume or sell.

158. Because soil acts as a carbon sink, disturbing it (as happens with building and ploughing) releases carbon. This is why it is so important to **practise "no till" measures on farms and in gardens** if possible. Rather mulch and cover soil.

159. This brings us to soil, a miracle that has made life on earth possible, and without which we cannot grow food. Yet we are running out of it fast, with estimates that there is only enough for about another 70 harvests in the UK. In this respect, planting trees is not only good for the atmosphere; by providing leaves and thus mulch, **plant cover can also feed and in fact create soil in the form of humus**. Thin, depleted soil than is poor in organic nutrients can also be regenerated by planting hemp and other green manures, which are then cut and dug back into the soil.

160. **Compost**, known as "black gold" by gardeners, is also almost miraculously easy to make, and equally miraculous in its effects in replenishing soil. The business of placing everything biodegradable into a compost bin, heap or hole, depending on whether you have access to a garden or soil, or feeding it to worms to make "tea" – a wonderful dark substance that perks

up plants no end – feels like the best kind of alchemy. The same goes for garden waste: I love piling up leaves, cuttings, clippings, prunings and watching them slowly disintegrate into rich mulch and humus that the thin soil in my garden gobbles up. If your garden is too small for freestanding compost heaps, you can get small composters – bins that will hold organic waste as it decomposes into compost.

161. Even if you have little or no garden, you can still **become an "earthworm farmer"**. Buy or build worm farm "kits" in which you place organic waste and a handful of wrigglers – who will miraculously munch their way through your potato peelings and torn paper, generating rich compost and "worm tea", which you can donate or sell. There are entire websites devoted to this topic that can tell you more.

162. Our own bodily wastes are going to become a significant part of the solution to rapidly depleting soil in the near future, so this is another reason, if you have the space on your property, to **install a composting toilet**. Once the contents of these buckets have broken down, they make excellent compost, particularly for fruit trees.

163. **Re-establishing biodiversity** – the rich web of microbes, fungi, worms, insects, reptiles and birds – is perhaps the third part of this equation. Without insects, pollination cannot occur; and without pollination, we will starve as a species. Spend a few hours on the internet researching how to attract birds, amphibians, insects and other wildlife to your surrounds – and how to protect them once they're there. This is not a hobby for the idle or the wealthy; the richer, stronger and denser the tapestries of life (i.e. food chains) that surround us, the better off we'll all be.

164. This is also one of the many reasons we need to **abandon monoculture and return to mixed farming**. In wetter

climes, farmers are planting "food forests" in which the object is to mix numerous kinds of plant foods and crops, so that, for instance, taller fruit and nut trees shelter lower-lying bushes and shrubs. Mixed planting and food forests eliminate or greatly reduce the need for pesticides, and offer shelter to a much wider range of life than vast fields of single crops or commercial plantations.

165. Meanwhile right here in Lesotho, **keyhole gardens** were developed as micro versions of the principles above put into practice: these consist of a small circle of raised beds, with a central point, accessed by a narrow "keyhole", into which organic waste and water is added. These break down and feed the veggies growing in the surrounding beds. These are especially valuable if your space is limited, or you are not fit or strong.

I watched my mother transform a bleak, exposed, raw-earth Free State smallholding into a rustling, dense tapestry of life in less than two decades, by dint of these steps: planting trees (hundreds of them); feeding the soil (with every scrap of organic matter the garden produced and tons of manure); and creating swales that soaked up fast-falling rain and distributed it across the land. From the mountain that overlooked their property, we could see a forest springing up over the years – one that attracted animals (including buck, hares, otters, genets and even an aardwolf); ticked with insect life and was always alive with birds; provided our family and my father's students with vegetables and fruit from rich, dark, crumbly soil; held onto water like a sponge in dry seasons and channelled it safely during storms; and was always temperate, even on the hottest days. Not all of us can create this kind of biodiverse Ark; but if we have the opportunity, we should seize it.

THE FUN AND FUTURISTIC STUFF

The writer and environmentalist Barbara Kingsolver is often asked why she is so interested in the future: her reply is that "The future is where my children will live."

We can look indeed forward to innovations that might restore our planet to working condition, and supply jobs and decent lifestyles for our children. Researching this book may have reduced me to despair at times, but I also found plans, projects and inventions showcasing the best of human inventiveness and adaptability, that ranged from fantastic to bizarre to inspiring. Here are just a few:

➔ Solar panels floating on dams to generate energy AND slow down evaporation.

➔ Urinals that fertilise school sporting facilities.

➔ Humanure start-ups (this is where I'd buy shares).

➔ Growing food in the sea in the form of seaweeds and algae (another reason we need to stop dumping toxins and sewage in the ocean).

➔ Growing meat in vats, or developing alternative sources – pet food manufacturers are already looking into worms, for instance.

➔ Bacteria that eat plastic.

➔ Biodegradable, renewable forms of "plastic", including a model being made here in South Africa from sugar cane, and another in Mexico using cactus plants.

➔ Recycling systems that turn plastics into fuel.

➔ Coconut husks, avocado pips, coffee grounds: all these natural forms of waste are now being investigated as alternative sources of packaging, furnishings, and more. Avo pips are being turned into compostable cutlery; and the really good news is that coffee grounds (one of the biggest sources of wet waste produced by restaurants) are on the way to producing oil that can replace palm oil in food-manufacturing processes.

➔ "Light bulb" plastic bottles filled with water and fitted into roofs refract sunlight into dark shanties.

➔ Refugee tents designed to harvest water and store sunlight.

- Biodegradable drugs and medications that have no adverse effects on water and soil into which they're discharged.
- Tree-planting drones that "fire" seeds into soil.
- Material made from biodegradable citrus pulp that increases the capacity of soil to hold water by up to eight times.

And so much more. As Free State farmer Danie Slabbert says, after 11 years of "regenerative farming" (no tilling or ploughing, no pesticides or chemicals), with the result that his land holds water better, and the quality and yield of his crops has improved: "You won't believe how nature can heal itself."

"Light bulb" plastic bottles filled with water and fitted into roofs refract sunlight into dark shanties.

CONCLUDING THOUGHTS: DECKCHAIRS ON THE *TITANIC*

Writing this book, I had some fascinating conversations with environmental activists, journalists and researchers, about the great conundrum that reading up on waste faced me with: given the multitude of ways we've wrecked the planet almost past repair, is there any point in reducing waste? Isn't asking people to give up plastic toothbrushes a bit like rearranging the deckchairs on the *Titanic*? In fact, polishing the brass screws on those deckchairs?

Leonie Joubert, the science writer I often cite, has pointed out that the only alternative to literally suicidal despair is to become solution-oriented. This has several benefits, and not just the obvious one – that concerted efforts by many individuals can have a significant impact, as we all learned during Cape Town's water crisis. Doing something, no matter how small, reduces our sense of anxiety, despair, helpless rage and grief. It also models decent behaviour for our children (who are going to judge the hell out of us – in fact, they're already doing so).

There is also the sense of self-reliance that going green gives us, as we learn skills (and teach them to our children) that will make us more independent, less needy and therefore less of a drain on our immediate environment.

To go back to the *Titanic* example: if the ship is going down anyway, it might not do any good rearranging the deckchairs, much less wiping specks of dust off them. But hastily roping them together to create extra life-rafts? Can't hurt, might help, and will give passengers something proactive and constructive to do in the face of impending disaster. Even better if folk pull together as a team in the process.

Now is the time to think collectively and act co-operatively, according to Lindiwe Ngwevela, a student activist. There is a new sense of urgency, a recognition (as Mozambique is battered by unprecedented cyclones, African countries reel under successive droughts and floods, entire ice-shelves disappear overnight, wildfires ravage California and Australia year after year, "freak" storms that claim lives become regular occurrences) that climate change isn't in the near future: it's already here. Photos of luxury cars washed onto beaches during flooding in Durban in 2019 indicate that even the rich are starting to feel the effects (which is sadly what it takes to get folk to sit up and pay attention).

Environmental reporting has moved front and centre, with a belated recognition that this IS vitally important political and economic news, not a "nice-to-have" option.

The silver lining to the apocalypse is seeing how people are responding to what is the greatest threat to the entire planetary population and its cultures. Amid all the (appropriate) horror and despair, there is a great deal of kindness and grace. I keep finding wonderful people doing extraordinary things. As we move to lifestyles where we're making more conscious and creative choices about how we use the world's resources, we're finding that hanging around solution-oriented people is good not just for the planet, but for our souls.

Just some small examples: on a cloth and clothing recycling Facebook group, I stumbled across someone who uses donated wedding dresses to make gowns and "pockets" (she doesn't use the word "shroud") for stillborn babies to be buried or cremated in. She makes these tiny exquisite garments for love. This kind of project might have only a small impact in terms of the planet, but as a form of recycling that showcases our capacity for compassion, connection and creativity, it's hard to beat.

In a similar vein, an endearing suggestion courtesy of writer Paige Nick: if you have athletic or scholastic medals rattling round in a drawer, Red Cross Children's Hospital in Cape Town gives every child who undergoes surgery a medal afterwards. They're calling on citizens to donate their old medals so that they can keep this lovely gesture going.

Another small local project: Cape Town writer Helen Brain has started a group that makes washable re-usable menstrual and maternity pads. She collects tatty old towels and T-shirts, flannel nighties and PJs past their sell-by date and uses them as filling. Obviously, some of the fabric used is bought new, but as a double-impact form of waste-recycling, this is a personal favourite of mine. Both disposable pads AND clothing too beat-up to donate to charity are kept out of landfills, but the real value of the project might be the sense of connection between the women who gather to make the pads, and the women to whom they're donated.

This is perhaps the strangest thing about the coming apocalypse: that it creates these connections and synergies. To survive, we'll need to re-engage with both our neighbours and our natural world. As Leonie Joubert has said: "To change the cultural narratives driving over-extraction and climate collapse, we need to reconnect with nature, and find measures of 'wealth' and wellbeing that are about communion with nature rather than hoarding stuff. Get ourselves back into the cathedral of nature, rather than the cathedral of shopping malls."

I wish all readers well on their journey towards waste-wise practices, and I hope it doesn't seem frivolous to express the wish that you have fun on your journey. Above all, keep sharing your ideas, tips, strategies. I look forward to seeing you on deck, lashing the chairs together.

If the ship is going down anyway, it might not do any good rearranging the deckchairs, much less wiping specks of dust off them. But we can rope them together to create extra life-rafts.

RESOURCES

SHOPPING CHECKLIST

→ Where are your nearest waste-free shops, stores and cafes?

→ Where and when are your nearest markets?

→ Where is your nearest community veg garden or neighbourhood farm?

→ Is there an active community exchange or freecycling organisation nearby? See www.community-exchange.org and www.freecycle.org.

→ Are there other resources (libraries, including toy and tool libraries, repair centres, bartering or co-op clubs, stokvels and so on) in your neighbourhood? This can be as simple and personal as giving your neighbours some of the jam you make with fruit from their tree.

→ To check the true green standing of whatever goods you want to buy, visit www.lazyenvironmentalist.com. Note that many of these products aren't necessarily available in South Africa, but the website Twyg gives good local advice: www.twyg.co.za.

→ For checking whether or not local products contain palm oil, this post explains the issues and supplies the database (regularly updated): medium.com/@nopalmoilza/a-list-of-palm-oil-products-in-south-africa-a5b87461b5f4.

→ For an enlightening (and entertaining) book on locavore living, read Barbara Kingsolver's *Animal, Vegetable, Miracle* about her family's year of locavore eating in Kentucky. Here in many regions of South Africa, we're lucky in that locavore eating is fairly easy, and often the cheapest, most nutritious and delicious option.

DECLUTTERING CHECKLIST

→ What NPOs and charity shops that receive used goods are near you?

Which will take your:
→ clothes in good condition (most charity shops)
→ clothing, towels, blankets and other textiles in poor condition (some animal charities, to use for bedding, some collectives that make hot or "hay" boxes, projects making re-usable menstrual and maternity pads)
→ old spectacles and medical equipment (St John Ambulance)
→ books (many charity shops)
→ toys and sporting equipment (schools and crèches)
→ fabric and craft remnants (community employment collectives)
→ furnishings (crèches, homeless shelters, shelters for refugees and/or families fleeing domestic violence)

RECYCLING CHECKLIST

→ Does your suburb or estate offer recycling pick-up along with waste removal?

→ If not, is there an inexpensive private pick-up option in your neighbourhood, preferably a job-creating scheme?

→ Is there an NPO nearby where you can drop off your recycling?

→ Where is your nearest dump, and what recycling options does it offer?

→ Does your local dump accept organic waste and garden refuse for mulching?

→ If you're unable to compost, is there a pick-up service in your
neighbourhood for organic waste?

→ What are your options for disposing of e-waste?

What are your options for things that can't
be recycled or chucked in the garbage:
→ engine oil
→ low-energy light bulbs
→ mirror and automotive glass
→ poisons or corrosive items
→ medical waste, expired medications

NEIGHBOURHOOD CHECKLIST

→ What green initiatives do your favourite sports, hobbies or interests offer?

→ Does your estate or neighbourhood have an environmental group or committee? At the very least, you can sign up for their mailing list.

LISTS FOR AVOIDING FOOD WASTAGE

→ What's in the pantry? Fridge? Freezer?

→ What needs using up today/in the next 24 hours/in the next three days?

HELP WITH PLASTIC WASTE

→ For how to help save the oceans from plastic, see theoceancleanup.com.

→ For more information on how to keep plastic out of our seas, and instructions on how to make ecobricks, visit www.aquarium.co.za/blog/entry/how-to-make-ecobricks-reducing-waste-at-home.

→ For an excellent and clearly written blog on the impact of plastic waste, read blog.nus.edu.sg/plasticworld.

→ For South Africans looking for single-use-plastic alternatives, visit www.facebook.com/SUPAlternatives.

HELP WITH WATER

→ To learn how to save water and use it wisely, read my book: www.bookstorm.co.za/books/101-water-wise-ways.

OTHER ONLINE GROUPS AND RESOURCES

There are literally tens of thousands of websites, blogs and social media groups that can help you on your low-impact-living path. Here are a few ideas to get you started, but choose what works best for you and your family.

→ Pick a few, otherwise you'll be overwhelmed.
→ Try to find ones that have practical tips and solutions to everyday problems or concerns.
→ If you're signing up for social media groups, choose ones that are as specific and close to your context (weather, locality, history, resources) as possible.
→ Stay away from conspiracy theorists and those who post only unbearably bleak prognostications, no matter how accurate these are: despair can be both catching and paralysing.
→ Make sure you have a decent fact-checking site for when you see claims that seem a bit dodgy: I recommend Snopes (www.snopes.com) and Africa Check (africacheck.org).
→ It's a good idea to pick sites and blogs that reflect your particular interests and activities – from hiking to cooking to commuting; it should be something that floats *your* boat:

- The granddaddy of green movements: www.greenpeace.org/africa/en.
- For an Africa-centred organisation fighting climate disruption: 350africa.org.
- For information on how to divest from extractive and fossil fuel energy: fossilfreesa.org.za.
- For an African NPO dedicated to disaster relief, especially in the wake of tragedies caused by climate disruption (cyclones, droughts, fires): giftofthegivers.org.

→ Pick people who inspire you and bookmark their websites or follow their social media pages. These are a few of my favourite "green gurus":

- For consistently brilliant, brave and entertaining green science writing, I read leoniejoubert.co.za.
- For her holistic, gentle and radical path-finding, I follow Mmatshilo Motsei and read her books.
- For days when I can cope with bracing but brilliantly articulated truths, I read Kevin Bloom (for South African analysis) and George Monbiot (for an international perspective).
- If you have waste and water-wise tips of your own to share, please write to me via my green blog: www.helenmoffett. com/green-hat.

ACKNOWLEDGEMENTS

So many people helped me write this, it's impossible to name them all, especially as many of them educated and enlightened me in the form of their words crossing my screen – a comprehensive bibliography of all the books, essays and articles that I found useful would be almost as long as this book itself. Then there are the hundreds, if not thousands, of people whose comments on various waste-wise or anti-consumer or energy-saving social media groups have been a constant source of ideas and tips.

I am nevertheless going to try to give at least some thanks and praise where it is due. While I waft around telling people to brush their teeth with bicarb and bamboo, there is a tribe of dedicated writers, researchers, scientists, activists and journalists doing the heavy lifting; who explain the complexities of the issues involving waste and the larger context with dedication, nuance and integrity, never losing sight of the bigger picture as they untangle fine points in their quest to educate their fellows, and to respect and nurture the environment that sustains us all. Lesley Green, Mandi Smallhorne Kraft, Kevin Bloom, Liz Mackenzie, Brenda Martin, Nazeer Sonday, Ryan Fortune, Brendan Abdinor, Vishwas Satgar, Mmatshilo Motsei: I am indebted to you for your commitment to green issues and the high quality of your research, writing, thought and investigative journalism on environmental issues. David Le Page of Fossil Free South Africa is always happy to spend hours discussing soil, compost and sewage with me over dinner (as others blanch). Karoline Hanks of Single Use Plastic Alternatives (SUPA), you walk the walk – thank you for what you do in our Noordhoek community. Leonie Joubert, your passion for green issues and headlong determination to make the world a better place inspires me daily, and the rigour of your research and brilliance of your writing always impresses me.

Thanks to Louise Grantham and Bookstorm for commissioning this book, for believing in its underlying principles ("these issues are not going away", says Louise), and for another experience of smooth and cheerful production. Russell Clarke gets 'flu every time he manages one of my manuscripts, but never loses his sense of humour. Credit goes to Nicola van Rooyen for marketing, to Sean Fraser for proofreading (and noises of encouragement), and to Marius Roux for once again producing such beautifully designed pages. Kelly Norwood-Young edited the manuscript swiftly and skilfully, and put up with being teased for her ever-so-polite suggestions for changes (I am more accustomed to the "What were you smoking when you wrote this?" school of editing).

The following kind people all gave tips, ideas and cheerleading when necessary, often via my blog or Facebook page: Steve Anderson, Diane Awerbuck, Erina Botha, Helen Brain and the Cape Town Washable Menstrual Pad Sewing (CWAMPS) group, Karina Brink, Nechama Brodie, Ted Botha, Christine Coates, Susanna Coleman, Mandy Collins, Mike Cope, Nerine Dorman, Grethe Fox, Leonard Gardner, Jane Griffiths, Bruce Hooke, Anthony and Stanley Hungwe, Gail Jennings, Billy Kennedy of Temenos Retreat Centre, Megan Kerr, Jade Khoury of Low Impact Living, Rupert Koopman, Rosa Krauss, Jacqui L'Ange, Kim Larsson Laria and her family, Helen Laurenson, Joanne Macgregor, Jill Mackay, Sindiwe Magona, Samuel Marimba, Julia Martin, Jackie May of Twyg, Sue Mottram, Lindiwe Ngwevela, Fiona Nicolson, Lovemore B. Office, Justin Phillips, Kate Sidley, Charlene Smith, Marianne Thamm, Margie Tromp, Bernelle Verster, Melissa Volker, Merina Wolmerans, Justin Youens and Rachel Zadok. Apologies to those I've inadvertently left out.

Annu Kekäläinen, Elisa Savelli of Uppsala University and Talya Tibbon all interviewed me for projects of their own, which helped me to formulate and clarify my ideas.

My parents, to whom this book is dedicated with love and gratitude, and my sister and niece, you have been wonderfully supportive. Thank you, Rodney and Dinah Moffett, and Kathy and Lauren Wootton. Lauren, you are a major reason I write these books: to borrow Barbara Kingsolver's words once more, I care about the future because it is where you will live.

Finally, I couldn't write a book – ANY book – without Paige Nick, who reads all my draft manuscripts, and then gives me honest feedback. Thank you for your edits on this, and for laughing at my jokes. You are my Everywoman reader, and I owe you forever.

PS: I managed not to mention my cats. Oh wait …

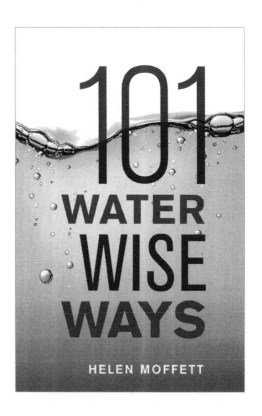

Also available by Helen Moffett

BOOKSTORM